How To Be

Genuinely Happy

Harnessing the power within

Tamela Duncan, LCSW

To my sons who have made me strive to be a better person in this life. To my clients who help me reach to find answers and to know greater compassion

.

Table of Contents

Acknowledgements

I honor and thank the many teachers, authors and dreamers who awakened my thoughts and imprinted my soul. To Lisa Fugard for her skill with content editing, her continuous support, and consistent encouragement, tenderness and kindness that kept me moving forward and believing in myself. To copy editor Lois Weston-Bernstein, who gently and diligently provided knowledge and persistence with the details. She is a gift to this project. With much gratitude, I thank Theresa DeAveiro for her technical support; patience and kindness (especially for those moments the computer and I declared all-out war on one another). I gratefully thank Doug Ghering for his talents providing creativity and assistance in cover design. Words cannot express my appreciation to my family, friends, clients and colleagues who continually asked about my work and remained excited about the finished product.

Rules for Being Human

(Handed down from ancient Sanskrit)

1.   You will receive a body. You may like it or hate it, but it is yours for your time on earth.

2.   You will learn lessons. You are enrolled in a full-time, informal school called life.

3.   A lesson is repeated until it is learned. A lesson will be presented to you in various forms until you have learned it. When you have learned it, you can go to the next lesson.

4.   There are no mistakes, only lessons. Growth is a process of trial and error—experimentation. The "failed" experiments" are as much a part of the process as the experiments that ultimately "work."

5.   Learning lessons does not end. There is no part of life that does not contain lessons. If you are alive, there are lessons to be learned.

6.   "There" is no better than "here." When your "there" has become "here," you will simply obtain another "there" that will again look like "here."

7.   Others are merely mirrors of you. You cannot love or hate something about another person unless it reflects something you love or hate about yourself.

8. What you make of your life is up to you. You have all the tools and resources you need. What you do with them is up to you. The choice is yours.

9. Your answers lie within you. The answers to life's questions lie only inside you. All you need to do is look, listen and trust.

10. You will forget all of this.

Introduction

Because we are born into a human body, we will love deeply, suffer profoundly, and spend many days in utter confusion. Life will present us with ups and downs, heartaches that will bring us to our knees, and joys we hope will linger forever. We will spend our lives chasing rainbows and running from the clouds. Trauma, loss and grief will leave us searching for answers, and our pasts will create our futures if we aren't consciously aware. Depression, fear and anxiety will give us the opportunity to learn lessons, and our natural inclination will be to avoid those lessons. "The Rules for Being Human" are fairly cut and dried; embracing those rules isn't easy, but the journey can be beautiful.

The complexity of being human can feel overwhelming because we have been programmed with teachings in our past, we live with struggles and emotions in the present and reach for dreams in the future. Few things are simple, and because of this, I've spent my life trying to understand human behavior. How does the brain work? How do we fall in and out of love? Why do people hurt each other, why do they hate, why do some heal from wounds of the past and others don't? Is there a higher power and why do some believe in it and others do not? How do you heal from the death of a loved one; how do you mend a broken heart? And how do you obtain real peace while living in your body on this earth?

My search has been for professional reasons, but it was born out of personal pain. I understand confusion, despair, depression, anxiety, and fear all too well thanks to a childhood dominated by an alcoholic stepfather and his raging abuses. In my naïveté, I assumed getting away from the things that caused my wounds would heal my pain. So as soon as I was of age, I escaped to an intellectual pursuit of college as a way to remove myself from my family and my past, at least temporarily. Geographic distance did help, but it didn't heal me, it only confused me, because, in spite of the pain of my childhood, I loved my family. And even with hundreds of miles between us, I was still suffering. Continuing pain and the recognition that I was repeating some of those cycles, created a desire to heal my life. When distance and education didn't bring me peace, I concluded surely therapy would, so I began a several year journey of self-actualization. Therapy helped, it changed me; it put my life in perspective and kept me from repeating cycles of my past. But I can't, in all honesty, say therapy alone healed me either. I am a fan of therapy, so much so that I became a therapist. I love the field and believe in it almost more than anything else in this life. But deep wounds cut into the soul of a human being inflicted in early childhood are hard to repair. By all plausible measures, looking back on my childhood, I should be damaged for life. But I made it out of the darkness because getting over it became my passion in life.

Following graduate school and much therapy, I got my legs of sanity under me and started my career. Then both my mother and father (though years divorced) were diagnosed with cancer and died within three months of each other. That was more than a minor setback for my sanity, as now, not only was I deluged with grief, I was immersed in family. The pain and sorrow of their dying processes opened the Pandora's Box of my childhood, and there I was, feeling it again. The result for me was more therapy, more reading and more searching. I grew. I soared in ways I never thought possible. Suffering has a way of catapulting growth when we allow it. And only a few years later my younger sister, who was my biggest fan in life, was diagnosed with terminal cancer and died four months later. Now I knew despair. Nightly, I lived in the bowels of depression, and by day I agonized over everything I had ever known or believed in.

I hated feeling miserable but pretending I was fine. I hated lying in the sludge at the bottom of the barrel, not knowing how to get up. I pushed through each day continuing to work at my job, parenting my children, and trying to do the things in life I was "supposed" to do, all while feeling like I had a five thousand pound weight around my neck. I knew I had to keep living, but I didn't want to do it while feeling so miserable. So I worked harder, even when I had to fake my daily existence more days than not.

One night while moaning and sobbing in my sleep, I had a dream that planted a seed of hope in my heart. A radiant silhouette appeared before me and softly whispered, "Choose Happiness, Choose Happiness." In my delirium, I reached for the pen and pad that rested on my night table, jotted the words "Choose Happiness" and returned to the void of sleep. I didn't remember the dream until I saw the sticky note on my side table later the following day. While sitting on my screen porch staring out into emptiness, I clutched the note in my hand, and vividly recalled the silhouette from my dream. As I pondered the words "Choose Happiness," calm and serenity washed over me.

What it eventually meant to me was that I could choose to focus on suffering and drown in that emotion or I could face what life had given me and see the gift, even in the pain. I could choose to focus on my broken heart or I could get up and be part of the world. I could allow my life to be dominated by wounds of the past and present, or I could work through it and make the most of what I had. I had a choice; not about the past or the control of disease and death, but I could choose how I experienced hurtful events which were out of my control. I figured out the secret of joy is not in joy itself; the secret is how you manage emotions that aren't joyous. So, I made a choice. I chose to stop wallowing and actually put effort into living every day to the fullest whether it was lived in emotions that were desired or undesired. That's how true joy was awakened in me. I learned to genuinely tap into my soul.

I had done enough therapy and sustained enough wounds to know there is more to healing than the psychological warfare that dominates the mind. My personal journey, constant reading, and soul-searching led me to a broader more holistic approach. I believe there are three aspects to the human psyche that determine actual healing, whole health, and letting go. There is the *biological,* specifically the brain, its cells, wiring and chemicals. It's the part of us that releases serotonin, dopamine, and stress hormones. There is the *psychological* which is the intellect, ego, emotions, experience, prior teaching and wounds. The mind, the thinking center, can help us or hurt us depending on our thoughts. Then there is the *spiritual*, the soul. It's the place of our higher self— enlightened, awakened wisdom, the divine consciousness.

Our earliest years start with the formation of *biological* brain wiring. One word spoken over and over, a child eventually repeats. We learn one word, one sentence, one story, one emotion, one judgment at a time. That brain programming is not just the speaking language you learn, but it's the emotional language of life that you eventually believe. One experience at a time, repeated over and over, creates wiring within the brain that creates your life. The journey of your neuron cells, though many of them genetically predisposed, takes information based on what's going on around you. We memorize actions, attitudes and behaviors and that memory becomes part of our future neural wiring. Like little roadways, maps of emotional and behavioral patterns are formed. Those roadways have created your thoughts, which create how you conduct your life. The *psychological* experience of your life in the past, and in the present day is constantly forming who you are. You think and believe based on what you were taught. What you were taught determines how you are wired. And then occasionally there's an inner voice that seems to come from a higher place of consciousness, and that's your *soul*. Your soul desires that you be the best you can be and that you live the life of your dreams.

These three parts make up the human experience, but the good news is that you are neither hardwired with how you have been, nor are you chained to the wounds of your past. Your thoughts, your brain, and your life can change as long as you put them to the challenge. If there is something in your life you desire to change, you have within you the power to do so. The gift is in understanding how to make those changes and how to make them last. It is a step-by-step process of understanding how you came to be who you are and how you can create the life you desire.

Chapter One

The Soul's Quest

"My soul is from elsewhere, I am sure of that, and I intend to end up there." — Rumi

Everyone has suffered. At times, everyone has felt disappointed, lonely, empty and even afraid. Everyone has had their heart broken, and everyone, if it hasn't already happened, will know grief and despair at the loss of someone you love dearly. The greatest gift of being human is that we get to feel, but many of those feelings will wreak havoc on our emotional health leaving us bewildered as to how to walk through some of life's hardest moments.

Being human is complicated, and beautiful. Sometimes we get to experience life at its best and at our best, and sometimes we experience it at its worst and as our worst selves. It isn't easy trying to figure out how to harness good energy when life is falling apart, but it can be done. Learning to pause, to go inside and ask yourself who and how you want to be in each moment can change a life experience. That takes skill and discipline. But even before skill and discipline, it takes courage. The courage to say, "I want to choose how I live in my skin."

I will readily acknowledge that my life has been altered by the experiences and heartaches of others. Each day I sit in a therapy office comforting parents who have lost a child, spouses who have lost their love, individuals newly diagnosed with cancer—fighting for their lives, families angrily divided because of conflicts, adolescents outcast because of sexuality, all the while trying to hold individuals and families together who are in despair. I've had the joy of watching heroin addicts overcome their compulsive desire to disappear from life to becoming leaders in their community. I've seen broken marriages fall to pieces and others experience repair. I've looked hatred in the face, held the hand of the weak and weary, touched the hearts of the lonely and frantic, felt on top of the world and at times exasperated beyond explanation, all because of the emotions of life.

Sitting across from me, a mother weeps inconsolably. Her tears cut through my skin and into my heart. She has lost her only child; a tragic car accident that has no explanation except, "It was an accident."

"Why me, why my son?" She wails in desolation. "I beg God to ease my pain, but it never stops; it's always there. I don't understand. I miss my child. I miss my child."

I can hardly bear the weight of her sobs and cannot begin to fathom what it's like for her. Regardless of how much training I've had; my helplessness to soothe her pain quivers right down to my soul. Her pain goes beyond the surface of our daily lives. I know the only consolation I have to offer is to reach in and appeal to her soul. Our emotions dictate our life, and our life becomes what it is because of our emotions. However, the soul is the pathway to making sense of the confusing emotional aspects of life, which appear so hard to understand.

Sometimes, the only recourse for our maddening emotions is to tap into the soul-seeking comfort of the heart to find that which goes beyond our human comprehension. Just using the word "soul" is tricky because it can mean so many different things to so many different people. The soul can be whatever you understand or need it to be, but for the sake of mutual understanding, I will be using it to describe your deeper conscience, the intuitive, inner part of the human experience. It is powerful, tender, loving, spiritual, strong and vulnerable. Regardless of the difficulties in trying to give it a label or description; its prevailing existence makes this human life make sense.

The soul, your higher consciousness, desires that you have the best possible experience while on earth. It wants you to heal, to be awakened, and to feel fully alive. It's the part that recognizes hatred, injustice, heartache, sorrow and knows compassion. Some are taught to tune into the soul at an early age; others are taught to give their soul to a higher power, while others are taught to ignore or stuff down the messages from the soul. The world we live in seeks absolutes, confirmation with provable facts, and because understanding and dealing with the soul can be ambiguous and subjective, we use all types of denial and avoidant behaviors to deter us from listening to its call.

The soul speaks to the human heart, brain, behavior, and wounds. When your mind is in conflict, the soul tries to help you work it through. When your brain is producing negative chemicals that pump through your bloodstream, it is the soul that tells you to get help. When a marriage has ended, death has occurred, or depression, anxiety, anger, rage, fear, grief and disappointment exist, the soul will try to point you in a direction to help ease your pain. The soul is what whispers in your ear, "Call a friend, seek spiritual guidance, call a therapist, or go to the doctor."

Listening to the soul is difficult because we have spent our lives divided between "believers and non-believers." Historically, the soul has been connected to spirituality, death or an afterlife. It is regarded as the immaterial, metaphysical, spiritual part of a being considered to be immortal. Conditioned and trained beliefs keep us from questioning our teachings about the soul as it relates to "God" and we fear the unknown. We get caught up in analyzing the spirituality of the soul, and judgments kick in. Who's right and who's wrong? Do humans have souls? Where does the soul go? Who gets to decide? The soul has been so entangled with indoctrination and the afterlife that we haven't been able to experience it in the present, the here and now, in a way that would benefit our lives. A lack of understanding has limited our ability to get in touch with the soul, so we're never quite sure what it is and when it is speaking.

Yet, we are constantly talking about the soul. Movies, books, songs, poetry, churches, temples, synagogues, education, science and even food speak of the soul. We spend our lives searching for our soul mate, trying to connect with our own soul and the souls around us. We go on spiritual quests, explore different religions, philosophers, and gurus hoping someone can show us the way to our soul. The soul is incredibly important to our existence, I believe, not because of the afterlife, but because of the journey we will take while on this earth.

Because we are born into a human body, we struggle. We struggle with emotional pain, physical pain, disease and eventually death. Pain in the body is not easy to withstand. Depression, fear, anxiety and broken hearts create equal amounts of distress. The mind and body suffer due to the multitude of biochemicals that will rush through the brain sometimes wreaking havoc on our existence. Our psychological thoughts will haunt us, others will be mean and unkind to us, and many times we feel helpless inside this human flesh. The soul is not only what makes it manageable, but what makes it wonderful.

What the Soul Knows

At six years of age on the Carolina coast, I first saw the ocean; a sight I shall never forget. My feet burned in the soft, luscious sand. I lunged toward the water then froze as the magnitude of the ocean thrust toward me. The resounding echo of the enormous crashing waves had me shivering in awe. The wind ripped through my hair, and there was nothing ahead of me except beautiful gray-blue water. Utopia did exist; I was standing in it. Mom pulled me into waist-deep water; assisted by the power of each wave, she hoisted me toward the sky. The July sun kissed my face, goosebumps from the brisk water encased my body. I laughed, clapped, squealed, made funny grunting noises and squeezed my mother in ecstasy. I wanted to cry.

I still have vivid emotional recall of the first time I truly "heard" a piece of music that wasn't from pop culture radio. I was eleven years old, watching a television Christmas Special when a woman began to sing *Ave Maria*. I couldn't move; something had overtaken my body. Heavy and limp, in fascination, I gazed at the screen. I could feel the music vibrating in my body, my skin tingled, and my heart beat faster. The piercing, transcendent sounds that came out of this woman exploded inside me. I wanted to hold myself. I wanted to float away; I wanted to cry. There was that feeling again.

The soul knows. It touches, hears and sees, and rises above the idiosyncrasies of life's conditioning. The soul reminds you that you are alive and that life is beautiful regardless of surrounding circumstances. The soul is moved by the beauty of emotions and experiences and awakens you to recognize what you may miss otherwise. It shatters your defenses and opens the heart. To me, it's what makes the journey of this human body worthwhile. Without the soul, I think of humans as being like Spock from Star Trek. Life would be fact-filled without emotional sensations; faces without smiles, eyes without tears, and hearts without feelings.

Everyone has experienced internal ecstasy, feelings so profound words cannot recreate the sensation. The birth of a child, an exquisite piece of music, the luster of a snowfall, or tender kisses, all sensed through the soul. These are the beautiful moments that wash sorrow away and validate our existence. And because of the power in those intense moments, we begin to seek experiences that move us and help us feel alive. It is easier to be in touch with life's jubilations when we are children. Defenses, skepticism and wounds numb us as we grow into adults and it becomes more difficult to bask in the essence of those precious moments.

The soul doesn't just ignite in exhilaration; heartache, loss and suffering are part of the soul's journey. It aches, weeps, desires, longs, feels ashamed, alarmed, and compassion. The soul is an array of colors—yellow, green and purple; and it's also gray and blue. The jarring of your tender humanness is the soul trying to get your attention. It's that inner voice that speaks when things are joyous, and when things aren't right with you and your world. In grief, loss and death, the soul allows you to feel the agony, not to cause you harm, but because of the love and passion you feel. It's also the voice of your subconscious that tries to get your attention when others are hurting you or when you are unkind and hurtful to yourself. The soul knows when your self-esteem is lacking; when you're guarded, defensive and fearful.

The heart is thought of in correlation with the soul. The heart falls in love, experiences lust, passion, pain and sorrow; yet the heart is an organ like the brain, kidneys, or lungs. They each perform a task to keep the body regulated and alive. So why has the heart been singled out as the emotional center of the human body when the limbic system in the brain is where emotions are produced?

The heart is poetic, with a romantic and emotional flare as it "beats with the rhythm of life." The strike of the heart can make you feel anxious or relaxed. When angry or scared the heart races. Breathing deeply into the chest and focusing on the heart can bring about calm. We can hear and feel our heartbeat, and we can feel and hear the heart of another. There are great passion and value to the heart center, and perhaps the soul does beat in rhythm with the heart. The gift is not in knowing what or where the soul is, but in how to listen to its voice.

Illuminating the Soul

The abstract nature of the soul, the fact that it cannot be defined, can create variance and confusion. There is alchemy to the soul that not everyone is willing to acknowledge, but everyone has a heart that's beating. Everyone has a heart that has been broken, a heart that is longing and, at times, a heart full of fear. It helps when we have a common language to lean on to help us make sense of this life. Either way, what creates a beautiful life within these bodies is the heart, the soul, the deeper level of consciousness.

We tend to leave ideas of the soul to the psychics, mystics, card readers, religions and spiritual seekers. But acknowledging your soul and learning to listen is required for you to have the life you were meant to enjoy. No one can tell you the exact way to be in touch with your soul; it's as unique as the individual body in which it resides. While there are commonalities to the soul's experience— compassion, wounds, love, heartache, grief and joy—those experiences are unique to you. Connecting with the soul is about being in those experiences and allowing them to cut the diamond from the stone. The soul is not merely feelings; it's the ability to be transformed because of those feelings.

We live in a world where humans crave intensity of experience. Reality television, Facebook and delving into other peoples' lives are almost addictions. We seek more, bigger, better, faster; be it danger, money, objects, or other forms of sensationalism. There is absolutely nothing wrong with seeking fun, joy and peak experiences; the issue is that it's never enough. What most are seeking is something to make them feel happy and alive, when ultimately everything they need they already have.

The soul is always present and available, but we don't always know how to listen. The soul doesn't come to you readily formed; your life's journey and how you deal with that journey is constantly adding to or taking away from your soul. It's always under construction. My mother sang this song by Joel Hemphill, to my younger brother, which lingers in my mind as I write this paragraph. "There really ought to be a sign upon my heart, saying don't judge me now there's an unfinished part." We do things all the time that either enhance or impede the soul.

Heartaches, losses, abuses, and neglects are in our lives to help form the soul. Suffering as just suffering is plain misery. There's no way around it; we will suffer. It's not the suffering that develops moral character; it's what we allow ourselves to become because of that suffering. I believe compassion and tenderness are often created out of experience. It's much easier to judge when we haven't walked in someone else's experience. Suffering opens our eyes to the shadows of our own souls and awakens us to the tenderness of another's experience.

I tell my clients when heartache and suffering ensue; they have three choices. Go numb, shut down, do nothing; this equals internal death. Become bitter, negative and resentful; this creates darkness in your soul. Or open your heart to be transformed by whatever you are experiencing; this strengthens the individual and the soul. Suffering can awaken the soul like nothing else on this planet—if allowed. The tenderness of pain allows vulnerability, creating space to nurture self and to be nurtured by others. It allows us to be awakened, forever changed. Nothing can take us deeper than suffering.

My younger sister was thirty-nine years old when she got the confirmation that she had liver, kidney and pancreatic cancer. I was basking in the glory of a perfect, sunny, fall afternoon, feeling joyous, when I received her call. When we finished talking, I dropped to the sofa, my arms tightly clutching my torso. I sobbed as I never had before in my life. I wailed in bitter agony. The pain cut through every fiber of my being. I felt like I was drowning in my own saliva, as animal noises eked from my vocal cords. I prayed, I begged and pleaded. "How can I withstand this suffering?" But I did, and I enjoyed our last four months with both pain and pure delight. I can truly say I was cut wide open, and I can honestly say I was awakened and in my soul as I had never experienced. My loss is not unique, as many have suffered similar and more devastating losses. It isn't about the losses; it's about what we allow ourselves to become in the face of those losses.

The heart can withstand great suffering with the help of the soul, but we often reject the opportunity for change, growth and awakening, because of the avoidance of suffering. We have actually evolved to believe we can avoid pain. Side-stepping pain means you will also side-step joy. We don't get to pick and choose our emotional experiences. We divide emotions into two categories, good and bad—the good we seek, the bad we try to avoid. In the spiritual realm, they are all simply emotions; not good or bad. Joy is only recognized as joy because you have experienced the opposite side of joy. One emotion leads to another and another. The highs will drop, and the lows will rise. A full range of emotional experiences lived in consciousness is the soul's path.

It's Neither Good Fortune nor Bad

Because we spend our lives focusing on whether things are good or bad, this determines whether we are happy or unhappy. We have a mental dividing line that tells us which side of life we are on from moment to moment. Feelings of anger, frustration and negativity often accompany suffering because of our emotional resistance to pain. Medications are administered in vast quantities to assist in the avoidance of heartache. And coping skills are acquired less and less to aid in moving through painful experiences. However, painful experiences are, and always will be, part of life. No medication or avoidance will change that. Turning to the soul and to the soul of others during difficult times is the only remedy to move through suffering. The soul does not recognize experiences as good fortune or bad. It simply moves through each experience knowing they are adding to who we are continually becoming.

There is a beautiful story (author unknown) about a wise Taoist farmer who knew there was no such thing as good fortune or bad fortune.

There was a poor farmer who had a beautiful stallion, but no gold. The village leader sent a messenger to the farmer and offered to buy the stallion. The farmer told the messenger to tell the leader he was sorry, but he loved his stallion, and it was not for sale. However, that same night the farmer accidentally left the gate to the corral open and the stallion ran away. The next day the village people said "Oh, you are a man of bad fortune. Yesterday you could have had gold for your stallion, but today you have no gold and no stallion." The farmer replied, "I am neither a man of good fortune nor bad fortune for we do not know the whole story yet." Weeks later the stallion returned bringing with him many wild stallions. The village people gathered and said, "Oh yes, you are a man of good fortune." The farmer simply replied, "I am neither a man of good fortune nor bad fortune for we do not know the whole story yet." Days later the farmer's son was thrown from one of the stallions and broke both his legs. The villagers gathered once again saying, "You are a man of bad fortune, for you have many stallions but a wounded son for whom you must attend." The farmer replied, "It is neither good fortune nor bad fortune for we do not know the whole story." Later a war began, and every able-bodied man was sent away to fight. Again, the village people gathered saying to the farmer, "You are a man of good fortune for all our sons have been sent away, but your son remains with you safe at home."

Life, its circumstances, and our emotions are constantly changing. As life transitions, so will you, vacillating between what you know as good fortune or bad fortune. Sometimes things will work in your favor and other times they will not. No one has good fortune all the time, and none will escape pain, loss, and sorrow. The farmer knew his fortune was not a matter of good or bad because in an instant everything can change. Whatever pain or sorrow you experienced ten years ago, five years ago, or a year ago, is felt with less intensity each day. Hearts mend, and we become stronger. And there will be another good and another bad, and another and another. Tapping into the soul helps you recognize them as experiences, neither good fortune nor bad.

Your soul evolution is about relearning and choosing how to be in your skin. It is a natural human behavior to repeat cycles, to do and become based on what you have seen. As we get older, many of us choose to change things about our lives. We make those changes depending on where we are emotionally at the time but seldom do people stop and think about changing their soul. Even the soul can be reconditioned or renovated to be what you desire. It is the single most important choice you can make versus assuming you are stuck with what you have been given. A song by Mary Chapin Carpenter beautifully states, "We've got two lives, the one we're given and the other one we make..." You will make a life based on what you believe.

Suffering, living in the bowels of depression and negativity, is often a matter of thought. Your thinking stifles your soul. The biochemicals in your brain are impacted as part of your thinking. How you feel about yourself and others are created out of thought. When hard places are present in life, your thinking will determine how you move through them. You will resist, or accept and move through changes based on what your mind chooses to experience in the moment. Your life's journey is complex, formed through your environment, biochemical and soul experiences. They are all part of one another, impacted by one another and influenced by your thoughts and choices. The power to change your life, heal your past and move with consciousness into the future can occur once you recognize the power of your thoughts.

Chapter Two

Your Power Is in Your Thoughts

"The happiness of your life depends on the quality of your thoughts." — Marcus Aurelius

We are always thinking. The mind is always on. In fact, you have between 50,000 and 70,000 thoughts per day; and most of them are repetitive. Even when you are not aware of your thoughts, you are having them. Your brain is wired, partially by your thoughts and daily life experience and your emotional health is being inscribed with your thoughts. We think our life into being as it is. Thoughts are powerful; they are the driving force of your happiness or unhappiness.

Some areas of science believe that our thoughts are cosmic; that their energies move all the way out into the universe. "Something, as small as the flutter of a butterfly's wing, can cause a wave on the other side of the world." One small change in a moment can result in large effects in another time and space. The power and energy of thought are indescribable. Everything in the world, as you know it, started with a thought. The automobile you drive, your cell phone, computer, the home you live in, the electricity, water and internet all started with someone having a thought. Paintings, music, mathematical equations, and colors are the compilations of thoughts put into action. And it's because deep, passionate thoughts and ideas are connected to the soul. Soul thoughts cause you to believe deeply and move you to take action.

The power of thought doesn't just invent things and produce outcomes; it determines how you feel about yourself and others. Thoughts form your moods, flavor your day, and design the image of life you are living. They decide how you move through disappointments, crises, and heartaches, how you feel about your job, companion, and children. You can't do anything without first having a thought. You won't go to the market, get a snack, pick your children up from school, or turn on your computer without your brain giving the signal first.

Thoughts are the starting point of having joy in your life; they can awaken you to tap into your soul. And thoughts will help you create the life that you desire. The energy of your life is being created from your thoughts because they eventually become your words and actions. This is where the power of thought gets tricky. Thoughts are learned; most of them are automatic without any level of consciousness and are often cyclical and dubious. Those pesky messages that you learned from childhood, that you vowed you would leave behind, are most likely part of your present thinking.

There is no way to escape it. The family into which you are born creates the base of your fundamental thinking and feelings. They dictate the language you speak, the faith you believe, and the knowledge and foundation of who you are. They also planted the seeds of judgment, fear, doubt, insecurity, esteem, love and hate.

Your earliest programming in life set you up to be resilient or fragile, combative or passive, to have faith in yourself or to be fearful and insecure. Whether or not you are comfortable with touch, live in shame, or are playful and silly, fundamentally started in youth. How you perceive the world, and how you believe the world perceives you, came through your earliest subliminal observations.

Most of us can say we have made many changes from the past to the present. But have you made the emotional changes that you desire in order to be the person you wish to be? You can make lots of external changes. You can change your location, looks, church, education, political affiliation, the books you read and the car you drive—trust me; I did all those things. But when your thoughts are riddled with verbiage from the past, when you are not living in your soul, or when you are carrying a heart heavy with wounds, you are not living to your full potential.

How Thought Creates Your Reality

Thoughts aren't always random or without power. Something in the mind or in the environment triggers them; they create accelerated energy as they roll over and over in your head. The most repeated thoughts are the ones that stick and have the greatest power in your life. You learn through repetition, the more you see or hear something, the more likely it will become entrenched in your brain. Before the "memory" capabilities of our cell phones, I had heard that if you want to remember something, repeat it nine times. So when there was a phone number I wanted to remember, I would say it out loud over and over. There are several phone numbers from my past I can still recall, but I know very few from the present because I recorded them digitally without needing to memorize them. Repetition establishes patterns in the brain. You have memory because the cells in your brain store information. The more you are exposed to something, or think about it, the more concretely the information is stored. As a pattern is established, it becomes automatic and easier to recall.

The more you cling to a thought, the more real it becomes, regardless of whether it's a true or accurate thought. Even untrue or irrational thoughts produce energy and action. Fears, for example, are derived from repetitive thoughts, and the mind eventually accepts them as reality. I had a client who said she would only cross a bridge which extended over a large body of water if there was a life vest in the car. She admitted that she had these thoughts over and over and circulated every possible tragedy through her mind. With great laughter, she described her fear as rational even though she knew in her heart it was irrational. She said she believed the bridge would collapse, sending her to a watery death of drowning. Just having a life vest in the car allowed her to feel safe. I wanted to suggest that perhaps a large hammer or metal rod would be a better tool to have so that she could break the window to exit the car, but I thought better of introducing that fear.

As silly as it may sound, this woman's fear demonstrates the energy and power of thoughts. You can convince yourself of just about anything—with repetition. The action of responding to a thought comes from the feeling the thought stirs inside you. That's why commercials and advertising work so well. The repetition of a food commercial stimulates the feeling of hunger and desire which prompts you into purchasing an item or going into the kitchen for that snack. If you think about something, again and again, it will ignite a feeling of anger, desire, jealousy, rage, joy, or laughter—it all depends on the nature of the thought. It is the plight of human nature to put repeated thoughts into action.

I had another client, (okay in reality several in this specific predicament) who playfully referred to herself as "the stalker." When she and her boyfriend were disgruntled or out of touch for what she thought was an unreasonable amount of time, she would begin to speculate that he was seeing another woman. As time passed, her anxiety would increase until she had to get in the car and drive by his home or his workplace in search of his car. She clearly knew this was irrational, but she could only be comforted by taking action. The power of the mind, combined with the need for the body to act, can and does dominate our rational minds. So, often in her pajamas, across town she would go.

Thoughts aren't always rational, and the mind can't always decipher what is real vs. what is imagined. And sometimes the more irrational the thought, the more we need proof because they tap into our feelings center. We tend to maneuver through life by the guidance of our feelings. Feelings follow thoughts. The more something stimulates the mind, the more likely it will feel real. As children we were afraid of monsters, the boogie man or some other made up character. No one had ever actually seen them, but to our minds they were real. We sort of knew there were no monsters in the closet, but most of us had to muster up the courage to go look.

Thoughts→Create Feelings→Create Actions

The power of thought creates feelings, feelings make us take action, and our actions stimulate the actions of others. How many times throughout history have we heard about one or two people who could stir and ignite an entire crowd? The words, energy and encouragement can convince ordinary people to take action. We typically think of this in terms of "the mob mentality" consisting of angry, reactive emotions. Hostile emotions or tender emotions can easily be stimulated by your environment. A seed planted in the mind can introduce a thought, trigger an emotion inside the heart, get us riled up and make us want to take action. We are moved into action by our emotions, but we always get to choose.

I know a young firefighter who was called to investigate a late night fire blazing under a bridge. What he found on this bitterly cold January night was an elderly couple hovered over a barrel attempting to keep warm. He was stricken with sadness at what he observed and felt he could not respectfully put out the fire. Upon leaving the scene, and informing no one, he went to a local 24-hour department store and purchased blankets, coats and gloves and took them back to the homeless couple. As the story leaked out into the community, others were moved by the act of kindness of this young man. People in droves gave time, charitable donations, and warm clothing items, impacting not just this couple, but numerous others throughout their city.

It takes one random act of kindness to soften the hearts of many. Emotions are built into our psyche, and what we think about deeply will activate those emotions. When the tenderness of others touches us, it stimulates softness within. It's our life's work to bring forth images and information that will provoke the best in us. *Pride,* a British film by Stephen Beresford is a remarkable true story about the struggles of one oppressed group reaching out to another and ultimately changing an entire community. It's a film worth seeing.

We are tribe people, affected by group energy. We connect, observe, unite, lead and follow one another. The reason social media avenues are so successful is because our survival and brain are conditioned to need others and to bond with like behaviors. As we follow, we become part of what we are following, which is why it is important that you choose what to follow wisely. A friend of mine teaches college and one of the things she tells her students is, "If you surround yourself with wise people you will become wise. If you surround yourself with negative energies, you will become negative." The beauty of creating consciousness in your life is that you can choose who and what you follow, and in so doing you are choosing who and what you are becoming.

As you are exposed to something over and over, that exposure becomes your truth, be it real or imagined. Your thoughts are constantly creating your truth. You will, in essence, act and behave according to your environment and thinking. Your mental focus creates outward behavior even when you are not aware of it. Not only does it create behavior in you, but it also sends a force of energy out into the universe. That force is then reflected back to you; it's like looking in a mirror. What you see is what you believe and what is real for you. The power of focus establishes energy, memory, intent and eventually action. When you focus on what you don't have or don't want; that's what you'll keep getting. If you desire change in your life, focus on that change. Set a goal. See it in your mind. Have good, positive thoughts around that goal. Visualize yourself changed in the future, but don't play mind tricks with yourself. You can't think a good thought for thirty seconds and then have your thoughts return to, "but I know it won't happen," because you just affirmed that it won't happen. That thought which you hold and believe deepest in your psyche is what you become.

Jim Carrey, financially 'broke," became depressed while trying to make it as a standup comedian in Hollywood. Being determined not to give up his dreams, he wrote himself a check for ten million dollars for acting services, placed it in his wallet and held it there for years, and continued to focus on what he loved. The check literally reduced to tiny pieces as it deteriorated in his wallet. Now, everyone knows the success of Jim Carrey. JK Rowling, author of Harry Potter, divorced, penniless and raising a child, was turned down by publishers twelve times. She is now said to be wealthier than the Queen of England. Dr. Seuss was rejected by twenty-seven publishers; John Grisham was rejected twenty-eight times. Walt Disney was fired by a news editor for lack of imagination then turned down three hundred and two times by the financial industry before he was able to finance Disney. Many recording labels rejected The Beatles, one even stating "the Beatles have no future in show business."

What all of these people have in common is they believed in something that was important to them. They kept their thoughts focused on what they desired. They didn't quit or give into self-doubt because of rejection from the world. They didn't accept defeat even when others planted the seed of doubt. Their thoughts became evidence in the form of energy and action. Thoughts created their reality.

You can manifest your reality by holding a thought and creating energy around that thought. As you learn to notice your automatic thoughts, you will see they are not as harmless as you presume them to be. When the seed of self-doubt is planted by you or others and becomes part of your thinking, it also becomes part of your internal energy. Those thoughts of doubt will dominate the power of your original desire—often you are not consciously aware this is happening. Years ago I was on a plane that had landing gear problems and was preparing for an emergency landing. The crew was amazing and, of course, everything turned out perfectly fine...except for my thoughts. I was in another city, so I had to get on two more planes to return home. Other than telling the story a few times, I didn't give the incident much thought...or so I believed. As time passed, I found one excuse after another not to fly. Before I knew it, ten years had passed, and I had not set foot on a plane, nor did I intend to. (Might I add this was truly not conscious?) Every time the idea of flying was presented, my mind made excuses or found alternate options that sabotaged me. Little did I know I was establishing a fear of flying with my defeating subconscious thoughts. I began to be conscious, and as I decided to pay close attention to my thoughts, there it was. I could not watch movies with plane incidents or news programs, without remembering the fear I felt that day as the plane prepared for an emergency landing. By subconsciously focusing on fear, I was creating fear as my reality. It took some work, and a lot of reality-check, but I started flying again.

The Freedom to Choose your Thoughts

It's difficult to embrace the idea that we can choose our thoughts, perhaps because we have so many, they fire so rapidly, and we have been told, "We can't." Thinking and the information within those thoughts are from habituation. However, you can learn to input new, updated, chosen information, create consciousness around thought and thus change your reality. I read that, on average, a person hears "no, you can't" about 150,000 times by the age of seventeen, and "yes, you can" only 5,000 times. Imagine if you worked on changing that. While your thoughts presently seem automatic, you do have the power within to change them should you choose.

The first step in choosing new thoughts is cultivating awareness. You cannot change a habit or a pattern if you have no awareness of it. Even when you have awareness, but are filled with doubt, you won't make those changes. If you are eating too much sugar, drinking too much caffeine or alcohol, or being a negative person, something has to bring it to your attention, and then you can make an intentional choice to change. You begin to problem-solve and devise a plan of how you will do things differently. You choose to limit intake. You choose to think differently about sugar, alcohol or caffeine, or you choose to have more positive thoughts. Perhaps in the morning, you usually start with two cups of coffee and then have a couple more during the day; now you make a choice to have no caffeine in the afternoon, but only in the morning. This decision is made out of an awareness of what you are thinking and doing.

We all have the freedom to choose our thoughts; most just don't know how to hold onto that thought and follow through with action. Begin with being conscious; listen to the soul or that quiet inner voice. Once you have awareness, decide, and become intentional. Decide what your action will be and then reaffirm that action over and over in your mind and habits until it takes hold. Behaviors and habits are learned, and you can add to or take away from any of those should you desire, and it begins with a thought.

The Power of Thought and Your Evolving Soul

While the soul is very much a part of our individual selves, it too has been affected by prior programming. Your expression of self, your courage or lack thereof, the fear and doubt you carry in your heart and your deep-seated insecurity impact your soul, and your ability to flourish. We will limit ourselves, squelch dreams and desires, and minimize passions in order to conform due to fear of retribution and

31

abandonment. When rejection or shame have been used to repress individualism, it's hard to come out of your protective shell. We are socialized, influenced by the actions and expectations of others. The soul wants to be seen and felt, the soul desires to question, learn and grow, but sometimes society teaches repression of gifts and individualism because differences create fear. And in so doing, your soul is silenced until you can no longer hear its call.

Your thoughts about your soul will determine what you believe, and how you live in that belief. Your thoughts about pain, sorrow, disappointments and heartaches of all types will decide how you move through them. The power of your thoughts will create your soul's journey. What you believe about the soul, depression, anxiety, happiness and choices are preprogrammed in your mind. The person you are presently was created through the imprint of your exposure. The person you are becoming can be created with your choices.

At any age and at any time, you can learn to get in touch with your soul. It is a matter of thinking and taking action—just as with any other change you desire to make. Bringing the essence of your soul into consciousness is the first step. Your soul is energy, an intuitive feeling that you know is real. Because your mind is so full of noise, demands, and distractions, that soft voice inside doesn't get much recognition. The soul is that tender recurring thought or peculiar dream that won't leave your mind. It's a quote or a line from a book or movie that plays over and over in your head. And sometimes it's painful interventions such as illness and other "wake up calls" that can't be ignored. You can hear your soul's essence by creating silence around those intuitive moments and allowing emotional space so that the soul may be heard. It begins by creating consciousness in your heart. You have thought your soul into submission, and you can think your soul back into its natural state of exaltation.

Wounds of the past will stand in your way. Your preconceived ideas create a sense of internal helplessness which makes healing and conscious choice difficult. Our deepest emotions are connected to memories of neglect, loss, abandonment, disappointments, addictions and heartache. We often don't know how to deal with those things, and they linger, define who we are and contaminate us inside. When our emotional needs aren't met, the mind and body both take a hit, and the soul suffers. We get cues from others on how to deal with gut-wrenching situations. And all too often, those messages are not convincing messages of how to heal and move on.

We need to be taught skills of resiliency in order to overcome helplessness. Becoming resilient, gaining strength and letting go of past wounds can be learned. When those around you do not have those skills, they cannot and do not teach them to you. A continued sense of helplessness is often carried from childhood into adulthood and throughout life. Learned helplessness is real because just like everything else, it is stored in memory and reinforced in daily experiences. When you have not observed the path of others who have healed, you have no blueprint to follow. By tapping into the soul and learning new skills, healing and happiness can occur at any point in life.

Where to Start?

Soul healing is about learning to align with your authentic self. It's about giving up the role of victim and claiming your inner voice. It's recognizing your defeating language and changing your thoughts. You know what you need, and you need to begin listening to those internal instincts. Empowerment begins with trust, and that slowly builds self-esteem; trusting your instincts, your needs and your inner voice. People want things to suddenly "be" better versus "doing" the work and putting in the time to get better. Just as recuperating from physical disease, emotional healing or change takes time and good care.

Through books, workshops, articles or therapy you can gain new wisdom and begin to embrace new insights as they feel right. You can make healthy choices that will heal your life. Begin to surround yourself with positive influences that will help you see the best in yourself. You can work to be self-taught by bringing positive energies into your life through reading, journaling, watching positive video talks, and paying attention to your thinking. Soul healing is about raising your level of consciousness and desiring a higher emotional plane of living. Your thoughts have kept you where you are, and changing your thoughts can change your life experience by creating self-compassion, one step, and one change at a time. By releasing your grip, and not hanging on so tightly to the story of your past, you begin to trust that you deserve to live a new story and a free emotional life.

Most focus on what they don't want and wonder why what they don't want keeps showing up. You have to realize your mind has been contaminated with doubt and fear, and those daily negative thoughts reinforce your mind and your life. Stop telling yourself the same old story. As long as you tell your brain that nothing is going to change, it will believe you. Your actions and your life will follow your thoughts and words. The power of the mind is dependent on what we subject it to. The story you tell yourself is the story you become. Even though you have learned your story from another, it eventually becomes your own. If you want to choose your thoughts and change anything in your life, you start by creating consciousness.

Your brain is waiting for you to tell it what to do. The power is in repetitive thinking; repetition will create an imprint in your mind. Thoughts hold energy in your internal body and in your external experience. When you can embrace the power of your thoughts, you will be able to create the life you desire. Change takes time, so be loving, gentle and kind with yourself as you move through this process.

Exercise: You are Your Story

Everyone has a story in their mind about who, what and how they are. We are our stories. We spend our lives walking around telling our story in one way or another. Others connect or identify with us based on our story. However, our stories have formed through time from images of our past, the opinions of others, and who we believe we are. You have a running monologue within your thoughts about who you believe you are, often filled with limitations, judgment, fear and doubt. You may believe that you are anxious around strangers, that you don't read well, that you aren't very attractive, that you can't learn computer skills, and on and on. Within that monologue you may have self-esteem issues; you may be defensive, short-tempered, or sarcastic. You have a story in your mind about who you are, and perhaps that story is hindering you from truly engaging in your life.

Let's start by taking a look at what you believe about yourself. Take ten minutes and type or write "Who Am I?" Focus on the parts of you that are tender and you feel could use some work. Be honest with yourself; no one is going to see what you write. This is for the purpose of self-improvement, not self-judgment. The thoughts are there anyway; it's just time to bring them into conscious.

Now, on another page write out "Who or how I desire to be." If you have a story that does not jive with the way you want to be living your life, describe how you wish to be in your skin. You may wish to take negativity out of your life, to be more happy and carefree. You may desire to complain less and be grateful more. Write out a descriptive picture of how you desire to be.

Compare the two writings and then choose how and what you are actively going to change in your life. You see, if you continue to cling to the first story you wrote, that is who and how you will continue to be. You should feel good about the story you share with others, and the story that lives within your mind. Your life story determines how you feel about yourself and the world around you. It is constantly developing your life. Choose a different story and become the story you desire.

Chapter Three

Brain Anatomy: Construction Ahead

"You have brains in your head. You have feet in your shoes.
You can steer yourself any direction you choose." — Dr. Seuss

You aren't stuck with your habits, patterns or thinking. And you are not stuck with the way your brain is presently wired. The brain is largely responsible for what happens with your emotional health, but you are the creator of much of what goes on with your brain's wiring. I stumbled upon something called neuroplasticity while reading about human behavior and it was a word that changed my life and my therapeutic practice.

The word neuroplasticity means the brain's ability to reorganize itself by forming new neural connections. Seeing the definition prompted me to understand more about how the brain can be rewired, at which time I began studying and attending workshops on the topic. As a therapist, this validated and instilled more hope and possibility for my clients. I knew my clients could and did change, and I knew it was dependent on how hard a person was willing to work. But what I didn't know at the time was how to fit all the pieces together as to why change was more successful for some than others. Now I know. Neuroplasticity is about altering or growing new connections and pathways in the brain through environmental and behavioral changes.

Changes in brain cells, their pathways, and in the synapses (the place where impulses pass from one nerve cell to another) occur due to changes in behavior, environment, thinking, emotions, actions and attitude. And if you think about it, you can change all of these things. The wiring in the brain does create how you feel and behave in life, but the wiring is influenced by the environment in which it is consistently exposed. Your repeated exposures, actions, and behaviors are what formed much of the wiring in your brain. It is done through repetition and what you hold true inside your mind as your convictions or beliefs. When you eat good food or exercise your body, your body will change. When you put new information and challenge your brain, the cell wiring will change.

Let's take, for example, your thoughts about anger. Let's say when you feel threatened or misunderstood your heart starts to race, your face gets red and your entire body feels angry. All of that emotional energy came from your brain. You justify those emotions by saying that is what happens to you when you get angry, and that you are wired that way. Currently, that is exactly right. Now let's say we do some coaching because you want to rid yourself of those negative feelings that happen each time you feel threatened. Think through the thoughts you have when someone is pushing your buttons. "That pisses me off. How dare they? Gee that makes me angry. I will not be pushed around, etc., etc., etc." The moment those thoughts start, the brain and the body jump on the anger wagon, and off you go. Again and again, you have carved a path of behavior in your brain's wiring until it seems normal. Your brain and body interpret a visceral, angry response as normal. So eventually you realize you are wired for that reaction. The same rule applies to jealousy, insecurity, self-doubt or any other unwanted emotional reaction.

Let's say you get coaching on how to relax and allow angry feelings to move through you. Then, the next time, something sets you off; the very second you feel a negative impulse—pause. Now, you learn to take a deep breath, relax your body—give yourself calming thoughts. "It's okay; there is no need to over-react. This is just a moment in time, and I choose to let it pass through me." And then you learn to choose different thoughts—it can be any thought. "I am grateful for my health, my life, my family, my joy..." or whatever feels tender in helping to release negative emotions. Anger, rage, jealousy, defensiveness or any other hurtful emotion can be retrained and released from creating negative emotional energy.

By understanding how the wiring in your brain works, you will feel less victimized by your life. If you believe your brain is overpowering you and there's nothing you can do about it, that's a pretty helpless feeling. But when you have the realization that you can make changes in your thoughts, and that will change the wiring of your brain; that's extremely empowering.

At any age of life, you can learn a new skill. You can learn to play an instrument, sculpt a piece of pottery, or learn a new activity. You can take on a new task at work; learn computer skills, new parenting skills, or the rules to a sporting game. This is done through putting new information into your brain and repeating that information until it is retained; that is neuroplasticity, creating new connections, activity, and wiring in the brain. The brain does not care what information you input; it will do whatever you command. The exact same principle is applied to new behaviors and attitudes. When you decide to improve who you are and how you live, your brain will adapt along with you. If you are a sad, angry, negative person, tell your brain you desire to be otherwise, but then begin behaving as if it has already happened. Input new good, positive information. Daily, live that new desire, and patiently wait as your brain becomes rewired to the new information.

Making the Connection: Rewiring your Brain

Everything in our body is connected, and we are connected to our thoughts. The point in understanding neuroplasticity is that as you begin to change the view of yourself and the world around you, the wiring in your brain is positively impacted and will change as well. I will admit the brain's wiring is extremely complex, and I don't understand most of it, but I do understand the basics. Although the wiring is multifaceted, a simple visual of the brain's nerve cells and wiring can help you understand how it can be rewired.

Think about the sponge-like melon that sits inside your skull. It's the central command station for the entire body. The brain's job is to constantly send and receive messages, produce chemicals to keep the body functioning and interpret information. Within that small melon, there are 1.1 trillion cells, and of those, 100 billion are neuron cells. Neuron cells send and receive messages to and from one another, to different lobes of your brain, and to your nervous system. Each of these tiny cells will reach out and attach to one another, communicating, expanding and growing. Once they are attached, the cell chain within your brain varies from a fraction of an inch to several feet in length. Here's what is so powerful. They attach and get stronger based on your actions and the repetition of information. In other words, based on what you do, see, and think over and over and over.

So what is the importance of explaining the fundamentals of your brain cells? It is important because they are connected to your emotional experience and influenced by your level of consciousness. Consciousness is your free will; it's self-awareness. And through conscious choice, you can aid and develop your brain's wiring in working effectively for you. It may seem far removed to believe that you can alter your brain's wiring, but when broken down into simple bite-sized pieces, it is comprehensible. We alter our bodies with our thoughts; because our thoughts are part of our body. It is imperative to realize that your brain and biochemistry respond to thoughts.

Below is a picture of a single neuron cell and a picture of multiple cells attaching and working together. Those tiny hair-like follicles attach to other cells, grow in strength and numbers based on your thoughts and experiences. Those bushy follicles are dendrites which are where information is received from other cells and then transported to the cell body. Starting with a single thought, followed by action, one cell begins to change, and then another and another. Cells can grow, multiply, stimulate energy and signal one another based on repeated thought, observation and action. I realize it sounds like a science lesson, but that is not my intention. I believe when we have an understanding or a picture in our mind, we stand a better chance of grasping the concept and making a change.

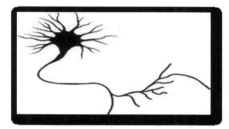 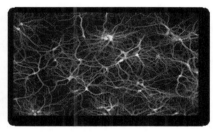

Single Cell Neuron   *Neurons attached & working together*

The power of a single cell is amazing; the power of multiple cells combined—astonishing. They have energy, they communicate, and they create who you are and how you feel. Your brain cells actually light up, they glow like a light when certain signals tell them to receive and fire off information, store information, or produce chemicals based on incoming information. Each of those 100 billion neurons will fire 10-50 times per second. And they can fire with the same old information or new information—it's up to you. The connections and command power of your brain is unfathomable to the human mind, and you have more to do with its potential than you may realize.

The power of your thought is food for your brain. The brain and the physical body have many similarities. As we learned to understand how calories, fats, and carbohydrates impacted our body's growth and energy, we could do a better job taking care of our food health. The brain is no different. There is a system of how it works, stores information, creates patterns, and how it can break cycles, grow new healthy cells and new patterns. This is how healing takes place, how resiliency is formed, and how you can have a life of joy regardless of past circumstances.

Think about strengthening the wiring of your brain the same way you would strengthen a rope. If you have a thin, single strand of string, it isn't very strong and can be easily broken, but if you add and intertwine another strand, and another and another, it is strengthened and becomes reinforced. That is what happens to neurons in the brain and how they will grow in strength and length. Your thinking and actions help create the structure of the wiring in your brain. The brain gets trained by the neurons receiving information again and again. Each time the neuron will store information more strongly and deeply in the cell. Then, as more cells hold the same information, together they form long-term memory and life patterns. This is how your brain became wired, and how it can be rewired.

Making radical changes in your life and choosing happiness is not about sitting in therapy and processing through your past, it's about learning how to let that past go and create something new. Once you decide to protest your current conditioning, wounds and limitations, you are taking on the task of altering your behavior and rewiring your brain structure. When there is doubt or disbelief, your brain feels it and falls back into old patterns because of its previous wiring. New wiring requires consciousness and consistent new thinking. Desiring to be better and learning to hear the voice of the soul can be your catalyst for change.

Hearing the Soul and Rewiring Your Brain

Albert Einstein said, "The intuitive mind is a sacred gift, and the rational mind is a faithful servant. We have created a society that honors the servant and has forgotten the gift." The intuitive mind is the soul. Those instincts that try to arouse change in you are often dominated by what you may think of as your rational mind. The rational mind may tell you that you cannot change. It will tell you your brain is fixed. Your rational mind will accept limitations that you have been taught. The rational mind will accept that teachers, parents or other adults told you that you weren't a good reader, or you were bad at math, music or fill in the blank. The rational mind will sabotage hopes and dreams, not because it wants to hurt you, but because your rational mind has been conditioned. Learn to honor and serve the gift of your desires and allow your rational mind to become the servant, stop listening to the old wiring in your head and start listening to your soul.

That soft, gentle, loving voice that wants the best for you is the voice of your soul. The soul has the ability to move you to a place of love and compassion for self. Your limitations come from your limiting beliefs. Your limiting beliefs are about a lack of self-love. Most spend their lives looking to the outside world for love and approval, not realizing that each and every one out there is also struggling with their own need for love and approval. Getting in touch with your soul is the start of an internal journey. Change takes place on the inside and works its way out into the rest of the world. When your heart's desire is to leave past wounds behind and move forward being the best person you can possibly be, you can be assured that is the language of the soul.

To begin, you absolutely need to stop thinking about the things that you no longer want. Thoughts keep neuron cells activated, and it is easy to continuously think about what you do not want. However, in order to change your feelings and behaviors, you must adopt new thoughts. Think about it in terms of your television set. If there is a scary movie on that is disturbing your psyche, you can close your eyes, but you still hear the scary sounds and music. So, your body still feels the fear. As long as that movie is playing, your brain is responding and feeling based on that information. To get it to stop, you have to either change the station or turn it off. That's what you have to do to rewire your brain. Stop the thought or behavior, and change to a new more productive thought. You can't keep thinking about something and expect it to go away.

Your soul is silenced by your negative, persistent thoughts. Once you bring your everyday thoughts into consciousness, you will be more adept at identifying those early conditioned thoughts versus your soul thoughts. The wiring in your brain can be most easily changed by creating space in your life to listen to the voice of your soul. Choosing to stay tuned to your soul helps your body and brain exist with a more positive healthy existence. That is the type of emotion needed to heal and thrive. The wiring in your brain will develop and respond to the energy in which you live.

The science of neuroplasticity has proven that you have the power to alter cells in your brain and to change anything about yourself that you wish to change. Old, undesired brain cells can be diminished, and new ones will grow with new thoughts and actions. Active thought keeps cells and cell memory active. New thought will grow new cell memory. Just as the cells in your skin produce new growth; so will the cells in your brain. As other cells are no longer reinforced, connections are weakened or eliminated; it is like sloughing off old skin. Through developing new healthy connections and pruning the undesirable ones, the brain neurons take on new formations and change occurs. Once you are able to do this, the life you desire is within your reach.

Chapter Four

The Power of Intention

"The only person you are destined to become is the person you decide to be." — Ralph Waldo Emerson

You will not, and are not, supposed to feel on top of the world all of the time. You will feel tired, at times down and unmotivated. Your body will naturally produce chemicals that cause you to feel poorly. Some days, for no apparent reason, you will wake and not have the energy you had the day before. At times you may even feel lethargic, irritable, quiet, emotional, or have thoughts of defeat. The chemicals inside our bodies will fluctuate, giving us more of one element and less of another. They rise and fall, working to keep us functioning and trying to create balance within. Biochemicals shift with hormonal changes, blood sugar, blood pressure, what we eat, how we sleep, and what we think, but sometimes they move through a natural change. Routinely, your biochemicals will shift just as the tide in the ocean rolls in and out. When they shift, they need your assistance to help with maintenance. You will run a full gamut of emotional changes month to month; and every now and then, day to day. It's up to you to create consciousness around your thoughts so that you can combat or override the difficult energies when they show up.

As you begin to feel the twist of emotions, and irritability starts to seep into your thoughts, pause and have awareness around what you are experiencing. When an emotion is grumpy or negative, pay attention; don't get annoyed with the internal change, simply notice. If you feed those negative emotions they will grow, they will stay around longer, and you will condition your mind and body to accept feeling this way. Cyclically, you may normalize being snappy, negative, judgmental or outright angry. That may be the internal truth of your feelings, but you can create consciousness, choose patience, good thoughts, or silent contemplation. With time, you learn that this emotional bump in your psyche will pass. Changing your thoughts is an important part of the process, and you can choose to be even more proactive by exercising or meditating regularly, and more specifically during these tough patches. Acknowledge that you feel bad, let it move through you and help it pass. As you learn to do this, you are creating a higher level of functioning emotionally and physically. If you learn not to fall deeply into the abyss of temporary misery, you will grow to be more in touch with your soul and become capable of embracing all of life; not only the glorious and good, but the somber and painful. Know that the tide rolls in and it will roll out again.

Living with Intention

The outpouring of emotions is powered by the input of thoughts. We can, and will, justify many of our emotions because we believe feelings overpower us, versus us being able to manage them. In so doing, we create and hold energy around emotions. We're angry because someone made us mad. We have no energy because we didn't sleep well. We're in a bad mood because, we're jealous because, defensive because—the list goes on and on. We somehow feel better about our whirlwind of maddening emotions if we can point the blame outside of ourselves. Anger, jealousy, defensiveness, holding grudges, depression and fear are all part of your emotional package. No one has to cause these emotions for them to exist. They can be fueled by someone cutting you off in traffic, the evening news, or you "getting up on the wrong side of the bed." We feel. We feel good, we don't feel good, we feel blah, and we feel bland. It's important to recognize that dark emotions are not bad; it's the power these emotions possess in impacting you that result in you believing they are bad.

When your intention is to project what you feel onto another or to get even, that's not a healthy feeling. When your purpose is to tear another down, it won't result in you feeling better about yourself. If you want someone else to hurt because you are hurting, you will only hurt more. If you feel angry or disgusted at yourself for experiencing difficult emotions, you will only feel worse. The suffering and conflicted emotions you feel inside are temporary feelings. They are not permanent, and they are not real; they are thoughts felt inside the body. They are part of your emotional wiring. They are learned from others, they are stored from past wounds, and they are a reflection of what you are experiencing on the inside. The goal is to learn to be with all emotions without judgment or despair.

Living with intention is expanding your awareness of self, acknowledging what you feel and deciding how to be in those feelings. You can create intention around your emotions by owning them. They are temporary, and with a little help, they can and will pass. Emotions that pour out of you and onto others continue to damage you. Likewise, the repression of emotions is as toxic to the body as overly expressed emotions. Creating intention is learning to have your feelings, and allowing them to move through you, which creates healthy living within. It is a very different action to allow an emotion to flow through you, like water moving down a stream, versus damming, holding and brooding about that emotion. Because we are inept in managing our thoughts, we believe we are powerless over our emotional health. Without awareness, persistence and practice, emotions can be a runaway train leaving you feeling helpless. If you truly believe you are helpless, then you are. Consciousness can develop positive intentions and change how you experience your emotional life.

If your intention is to point fingers at another, you will not be able to look at yourself. If your intention is to numb or avoid painful, scary emotions, you probably won't have a very rich full life. If your intention is to create drama and chaos, that will be the energy of your life. Even when you don't know that these things are your intentions, but you keep doing them, they are your intentions. But if your intention is to feel fully alive by experiencing loss, grief, joy and ecstasy you will have to take responsibility for the good, the bad and the ugly emotions. You will need the consciousness to know they will pass, learn to let them move through you, and evolve to know you are better for having experienced them.

Creating Consciousness

The antidote, to what seems like unmanageable emotions, is not to set yourself up to believe that you won't have them, but to change how you have them. We all have those periodic difficult patches, and at times we may also experience longer more trying periods leading to feelings of anxiety or depression. With consciousness, you grow to know your mind and body. Consciousness is about being awake, aware of what is going on inside you. Through learning to pay attention, you recognize your experience and see it for what it is without panic or judgment. You know when it's those rough couple of days versus when it's the heavier longer lasting periods of anxiety or depression. Either way, know that there is a struggle occurring inside you, and with consciousness, you can grow to work through life's hard moments.

You lay awake at night; incessant thoughts torment your sleep. You wake feeling tired. Day after day you know you don't feel right in your mind and body. You crave sweets, food or other substances to feed your weary disposition. You want to feel livelier and know what you need to do to make changes, but your negative thinking talks you out of them. You tell yourself you want to get outside more, to exercise, to laugh more or to have downtime, but you don't do it. Stress begins to take over. The negative hold is too tight, and you can't shake your feelings of helplessness. So, instead of doing anything positive, you sink deeper into the abyss of apathy. You engage less, criticize more, have negative thoughts and even feel sorry for yourself. Some may even go to a doctor and get put on medication to "help" them feel better. As you do these things, you are acting out of previously learned patterns believing you can't do anything to help yourself.

In order to change, you need to reinvent your present self with an image of your future self. You have to consciously think through how you desire to be and hold that image in your thoughts. Falling back on old ways is written in your brain, and your job is to override its programming. Your past is what your brain, body and chemicals know, and that is the image they will continue to hold until you establish and hold a new image. The power of intention is about intentional living, not preprogrammed living. Consciously see the person you desire to be and see yourself becoming that person.

You can't expect to walk through this life and never be depressed, anxiety-ridden or completely out of sorts with stress or anger. But you can expect yourself to walk through those times differently. As you experience situations of aggravation or heartache, your body will feel the distressed energy. Your natural inclination will be to fall into old patterns that are familiar to your physical being. To do it differently, learn to hear your internal soul that desires growth and change. To start, you have to begin living and seeing yourself as though you are not depressed. If you focus on the depression, that will be your mind and body experience. If you focus on an improved self, you will walk toward improvement. What that means is, imagine feeling better. Imagine taking walks every day, and then take them. Imagine laughing and talking with friends, but then do it. Your old image of self will continue to produce a depressed self. Create a new image and live as if you are healthier. Having a new thought, followed by action creates new behaviors. Then staying with the new action is required in order to have change.

Because we operate from previously learned information, you have to exert an effort to create a new way of being. Your brain believes what it has already been taught and that is what has created your life experiences. We live in the past and believe the past because the past is what the brain recognizes. It is information that you already hold in your head. It's already in there; you don't have to exert any effort. The past is automatically lived in the present. You have to teach yourself new emotional content, and with time, your body will begin to believe it. Most people want the body and mind to change without having to work for those changes. You can only change your future outcomes by thinking them before they actually get here.

Let me explain. If you feel depressed and your brain recognizes the reaction to depression as lying on the sofa—you will lie on the sofa, because you consider this behavior "normal." You reinforce the action by telling yourself that it will make you feel better. Even though it doesn't make you feel less depressed, you keep doing it. As you keep doing it, it is more strongly reinforced. Lying on the sofa will not increase your energy or your production of serotonin and dopamine, and you know this, yet you lie on the sofa. You have been programmed to take the easiest and most comfortable path available to you.

You have the option of creating a new method of dealing with feelings of depression, anxiety or any other type of distress. Suppose the next time you feel like lying on the sofa you choose to take a walk instead. You get out the headphones and plug in some beautiful music. You take a walk through the park, your neighborhood or even do laps around the gym. As you walk, you enjoy the music, you have good, hopeful thoughts and envision yourself feeling better. Your heart feels lighter, your energy improves, and your body begins to produce positive biochemicals. Now, suppose you create a pattern of this new behavior, and every time you start to feel low, depressed or anxious, you take a positive action. You are teaching yourself and your brain a new reaction to difficult emotions.

Change takes time; it requires repeating an action over and over until it takes hold. If you try a new action here and there, it won't take hold. If you try a new action for two weeks, it is highly unlikely that it will take hold. But if you decide to create a new lifestyle for yourself, it becomes part of who you are and how you live life. The actions required to care for your physical health and mental health are very similar. If you have high cholesterol or high blood sugar and you eat non-fatty meals or reduce your sugar intake for a week or even a month, will you have cured your health issues? Not any more than exercising a total of three times will produce weight loss or a fit body. Making a lifetime commitment to healthier eating habits will produce improved health. Making a lifetime commitment to being proactive with your mental health will produce a happier, better emotional life.

Change Starts on the Inside

Part of what makes change in the present so difficult is thoughts and wounds of the past. Most of us can look into our hearts and see hundreds of hurts, habits, and offenses caused by what someone else said or did. We also can look at ourselves and see perhaps as many that we have inflicted on others. It's a personal choice to move beyond your story of pain, negativity or helplessness, as they are limiting your life. Memories and obsessive thoughts have the power to cause as much, if not more, misery in the present as was caused by the past itself. You are in charge of your memory and your mind. I have four siblings who suffered many of the same wounds of childhood that I suffered. We each have a different story, and we each have a different life because of those stories.

You can spend your life looking back and blaming those that hurt you, and in so doing you will keep those wounds forever alive. Blame will never free you from suffering. When you are preoccupied with blame, you are consumed with looking outside yourself. Wounds are burrowed deep, change and healing have to occur from within. Your mental attitude will determine the outcome of your life as it sketches an image of you and the world around you for your brain. Whether you are working to heal wounds, let the past go, or making changes in the present, as you become a happier person, your brain will absolutely begin to change. Your daily activity, choices and thoughts can transform earlier conditioning. Thoughts have created the life you have, and they can recreate a life you choose.

Our mental health takes an emotional beating because of what we believe. Humans spend their lives creating stories that wind up dictating who they are constantly becoming. We all need to be acutely aware of the story we tell ourselves. Few things in life are as horrible as you believe them to be. The majority of negative feelings arrive from thoughts and not out of what is actually happening. Mark Twain said, "I've had many worries in my life, most of which never happened." Create consciousness and compassion around all emotions. Let them flow through you, learn not to let them dictate how you respond, or to hate yourself or anyone else because of them, and know they will pass. How you live your emotions is a choice, but you cannot choose without awareness. Happiness is about freedom; freedom from thoughts that create agony in the heart and distress in the brain and body. Being able to look at events in life and see them as events, occurrences that come and go, will alter how you live your emotional life.

Your soul desires the path of healing. It desires to be free of negative thoughts and to blossom into a life of joy. There are hundreds of disorders, diagnoses and syndromes to explain why we are the way we are, but the path to healing is pretty much the same for all. You are and have become what you cannot let go of. The story of who you are is often a myth created out of suffering. The story of who you become can be a choice rooted in heart and soul.

Become more in tune with your soul. The more you are capable of tapping into your soul, the more sense you can make of human emotions. Anger, frustration, intolerance and disappointment will be part of who we are. Love, compassion, forgiveness and understanding are also within you. Emotions get your attention; they make us feel alive. The feeling itself is not the issue; how you respond and live in your feelings determines the energy of your life. The beauty of being human is to have a full range of emotions, to experience passion, joy and ecstasy, as well as hurt, agitation and sorrow. It's impossible to extinguish or avoid unwanted emotions, but you can choose how you move through them. The soul can help you learn to regulate what's effective and appropriate if you learn to listen. Remember to pause and know your intentions, because the power of intention will open up a whole new emotional experience for your life.

Chapter Five

What You Think Can Harm You

*"Nothing can harm you as much as your thoughts
unguarded." — Buddha*

Thoughts can disturb your psyche, keep you from living a fulfilled life, and wreak havoc in your heart. They persuade you to feel grumpy, embarrassed or self-conscious. Or they can make you feel beautifully alive. Thoughts can weaken your immune system, cause your cells to get sick, and make your body ill. Whatever the subconscious mind thinks and believes, the conscious mind will create. When the subconscious mind is filled with negative energy, the body feels the impact. The subconscious mind is active and powerful; it runs your life. And still, most of us find it hard to believe that our thoughts can harm us.

Too often the voice inside our head is, "I can't." I can't lose weight; I can't exercise; I can't cook; I can't meditate…I can't. We sabotage our happiness with thoughts of inadequacies. "I am not smart, I don't read well, I'm not good with people, I inherited depression," and on and on. Your internal narrative has created who you've become and will continue to create who you will be in the future. The majority of thinking is subconscious and moves through your mind without your awareness. Consciousness is the first step in healing wounds, changing behaviors and creating a happier life.

I worked with a woman, Chris, who came into therapy because of a life of misery due to a fourteen-year history of heavy addictions. She was in Narcotics Anonymous, and although she had been clean for years, she still had tormented, self-loathing thoughts which made her want to use every day of her life. Alcohol use began in her teens, and numerous substances followed including cocaine and even heroin on a few occasions. She had stolen from friends and family to maintain her addiction, accepted abusive relationships, and had even prostituted herself in exchange for drugs.

Her childhood was not notably horrific in a way that would have led one to easily understand her life of addictions, prostitution, and self-hate. Her family consisted of what Chris referred to as, "successful, educated, perfectionist, overachievers." Money, accomplishments and success were the driving forces in her family. However, there were the everyday after-work cocktails, wine with dinner, and social drinking at all occasions. She referred to her parents and extended family members as functional alcoholics and "pill poppers." As the youngest in her family and often left unsupervised and isolated, Chris fell into years of boredom, fear and self-defeating thoughts. She never felt as "good as" her brother and sister, she didn't like school and didn't feel successful "at anything."

Chris began slipping drinks from her father's liquor cabinet as a teen in an effort to soothe the difficult adolescent years. Suffering from poor grades, social isolation, no ambition and shame, she moved into heavier and heavier substance use. She then began stealing painkillers, sleeping pills and nerve medications from parents, friends and neighbors' medicine cabinets. It became evident she would not be able to go to college, and her crippling self-hate grew as she believed she was "the screwed-up black sheep" of the family. After barely squeaking through high school, she refused to go to rehab and instead married her twenty-seven-year-old drug supplier and moved hundreds of miles away. A nine-year string of failed relationships, heavy substance use and estrangement from her family followed. There were a few unsuccessful days in rehab and attempts here and there at getting clean. Chris proclaimed the reason she finally wound up dried out and in Narcotics Anonymous wasn't that she wanted to be clean, but that she had a fear of dying and knew on her present path that would be the outcome, sooner than later. It was her Narcotics Anonymous sponsor that referred her to therapy in hopes that Chris could deal with her issues and remain clean.

Therapy for Chris was about unraveling her constant self-hating thoughts. She believed she wasn't smart, had no opportunity for success, and that no one "decent" would want to be in a relationship with her. Her view of herself was that she had "fucked up" her life, was a failure and always would be. She lived a life of obsessive self-tormenting thoughts. Chris believed the only time she felt peace was when she was "high." Truly that was not peace, but deadened emotions.

Our therapeutic journey lasted for years and was primarily about Chris redefining herself. As grueling as a college class, she diligently did the work. Regularly she journaled, read books, dissected her thoughts, worked her program in Narcotics Anonymous, and maintained consistent therapy appointments. She grew to understand and accept that the only thing working against her was her thoughts. Chris took accountability for the choices she had made; she learned forgiveness, the art of letting go, and began changing her life. She went to college. She repaired relationships with her family members and was able to see them as separate entities with which she had the power to choose connections that worked for her. Chris gave up the role of victim and powerlessness and created a life she desired.

I seldom see people with devastating mental illness or extreme disorders; I see people with contaminated minds. Thoughts create addictions, eating disorders, abuses, anxiety, depression, self-hate, low self-esteem, fear, doubt, judgment, arrogance and entitlement. They keep you on the sidelines away from opportunities and enjoyment. They create the bars that hold you imprisoned by a life of choice. Nothing will ever be more destructive than toxic thoughts. Thoughts are the single most damaging thing inside your body.

The Story of Two Wolves

There once was a Cherokee elder who told the story of life to his grandson. The grandfather told the grandson that in every heart there is a battle of two wolves. One wolf is angry and dark, filled with anger, jealousy, greed, resentment and insecurity. The other wolf is good and kind filled with joy, hope, humility and compassion. The grandson thought about this for a minute and then asked the grandfather, "Which wolf wins?" The grandfather simply replied, "The one you feed."

Slowly, the tender soul of humans is colored by the presence of negligence; the negligence of not teaching hope, belief, forgiveness and compassion. Beginning in our earliest years, we learn to feed the angry wolf until we are consumed by its presence. The angry wolf is typically fed to ward off what we think is the threat of another, but at some point, the wolf will turn on you and become your destroyer. Whatever you feel toward another, you will experience in your own skin. You cannot hate another without hating yourself; you cannot condemn another without living your own condemnation. The lens through which you view the world is the container in which you live. Your thoughts are constantly feeding your experience.

Thoughts not only hurt your sense of self, relationships, mental health and happiness; they have the power to damage the body. We feel our thoughts right down to a cellular level. There are cells in your body which are receptors; meaning they receive and become conditioned based on outside stimuli. When you are feeling loathing, fearful, angry, guilty, and resentful or any other negative emotion, a flurry of damaging chemicals are released into the body and onto your cells. Little by little you have trained your internal body by feeding it with your thoughts.

The Body Stress Connection

People can and do literally become addicted to stress, chaos and drama. It isn't a natural behavior of mankind, but a learned reaction. For example, when families are quick to anger, yell and fight, there is an adrenaline rush. The propensity for road rage, antagonistic comments and sarcasm are acquired over time. When there is habitual tardiness, anxiety, complaining and worry, young bodies get used to an overly saturated, adrenaline feeling. These heightened emotions come with a burst of energy that makes you feel like you can fight a tiger. With time, you normalize the feeling of fight or flight, and your brain and body learn to automatically release a flurry of chemicals as you have that feeling. As heightened levels of adrenaline are released day after day, your body begins to crave it. So, two things are happening. The brain and body become trained with the production and feeling of the chemical being present. And you take on the familiar behaviors you have learned and believe it is how to behave. This becomes the normal way to feel and live.

There are others who are exposed to a life of drama and chaos, who take on helplessness but show no outward response. Still, the body takes a hit. Internalizing emotions of fear, anger and anxiety can do as much damage as if the emotions were overtly expressed. There is still a release of an overabundance of adrenaline and cortisol. Thoughts are still racing through the mind; chemicals are still rushing through the body. Perhaps your conditioning has been repression; silence doesn't mean the internal body isn't being hammered with damaging chemicals. When emotion is not expressed or denied, it will take its vengeance on the body. When emotion is overly expressed or indulged, it wreaks havoc in the body. In both situations, it not only affects the body; it first wears on the soul.

The mind, body and spirit can be made sick, or well with the power of thought. There are many predisposed mechanisms in your body to overcome pain and distress, but your capability to utilize them is determined by the coping skills you have or have not learned. Take, for example, your adrenal glands. They are crucial for life as they secrete numerous hormones that regulate bodily activities, and prepare your body to respond to stress. These two little glands that sit on top of your kidneys secrete adrenaline, endorphins, epinephrine, cortisol, DHEA, aldosterone, testosterone, and estrogen. While the adrenal glands are programmed to secrete the chemicals that your body needs as you need them, they also produce them at alarming rates based on your thinking. As you live a daily life of anxiety, anger, depression, or unresolved issues, your body will be in a state of distress. Your system will eventually become unstable because of the ongoing release of too many stress hormones contaminating not only your mind, but your body as well.

If stress hormones aren't released and then dissolved by the body, these hormones tell other functioning parts of your body to react. Your blood thickens, heart races, blood pressure increases, stomach acid is produced, and muscles constrict. Everything from your nervous system, muscular system, brain chemicals, heart, lungs, pancreas and kidneys are affected by stress and aggravated emotions.

All of this impacts sleep, appetite, energy, fatigue, aches and pains, anxiety, depression, and overall bodily functioning. There will come a point when the body can no longer protect itself against these raging stress chemicals, and breakage occurs. Changes in your behavior can change this damaging cycle in the mind and body.

Resilience and Optimism

It's not a question of "can you think yourself better?" it's a matter of what your brain truly believes. If we could, every one of us would think ourselves into perfect physical and mental health and happiness. The conviction of thought is what powers the brain to produce outcomes. You can't trick the brain into believing that you believe something that you actually don't. Optimism held deep within your core creates an energy your brain recognizes. That energy stimulates the neuron cells in your brain to produce chemicals based on what you believe. Like everything in this universe, the cells and biochemicals in you are reactive. They are reactive to your thoughts.

Conviction of your soul is what gets your brain's attention. When the soul illuminates with resounding truth, every part of your body will benefit. If you pause and think for a moment, you can connect or relate to that deep sense of "knowing" or "feeling" something. Emotions of passion, confidence, tenderness, nurturing, empathy, and kindness that resonate throughout the body don't happen with careless thought; they are prompted and felt with an awareness of the soul. They are different than fleeting, busy, "monkey mind" thoughts. When a thought reverberates on a soul level, energy exists that creates movement. That movement is what lights up and ignites your brain and body chemicals. There is an awakening, a stirring of consciousness and your cells listen. Your mind, heart and body feel the difference. The soul is an intentional, knowing force that lives in the body.

One of my dearest friends, a mentor, and the person who motivated me to pursue the field of mental health, passed away when I was twenty-five years old. This was during the eighties when the treatment of cancer was fairly new, so Becky traveled near and far for hopeful treatments. Over time she realized her prognosis was not good and she worked to settle into some form of acceptance. Stricken with sadness, but trying to enjoy every moment we shared together; we were compelled to hash out as many of life's quandaries as possible. Our visits would go late into the night as we talked about therapy, spirituality, music, movies and madness.

During what I would later know as our last visit in Becky's home, she told me something I have never forgotten. She told of a woman she met at a holistic healing group in Texas. The woman had been given a grim diagnosis years' previously, but was in remission, traveling about and enjoying her life. Becky said her new friend insisted that she wasn't going to die anytime soon and was determined to get on with life. Becky, in her final stage of life, said to me, "I always wanted to get better; I just never really thought I would. Deep in my soul, I knew I wouldn't survive this." The next call I received, Becky had been hospitalized and only lived a few days.

It's our natural inclination to lose faith and accept defeat when told devastating news about our health. We can't help but be vulnerable to the words of the powers that be, yet there are some souls that meet detriment with resistance. Internal determination sets a mental tone for how you move through your life and live out your story. Optimism does not necessarily mean that you will survive a life-threatening disease; although sometimes it does. It means your body can feel and live fully alive regardless of information.

The energy of optimism changes a life. It radiates in smiles, laughter, seeking out the good and feeling internal peace. Resiliency is developed in how you internally process information. Information is information; attitude establishes the outcome of your emotional health around information. Optimism can create resiliency whether it's a situation of trauma, abuse and neglect, debilitating health issues, or anxiety and depression. You cannot change information; however, you can change your life experience in spite of the information. Internal resolve prompts the brain to produce the chemicals your body needs in order to overcome hardship. Determination, an optimistic heart, and positive thoughts create resiliency and generate outcomes.

Having an ideal, easy life is not the foundation of optimism and resiliency. Resiliency is developed through challenges and adversity. "What doesn't kill you makes you stronger," is not a cliché, it's a biochemical reality. By learning to be flexible, hopeful and persistent, resiliency is born. It evolves by focusing and holding onto the positives in life even when they are few. An element of determination, held with positive attributes, changes the process of the mind. Resiliency arises by not seeing oneself as helpless or a victim, and not repeatedly telling your story as though you are a victim. Your brain will carry a mental image based on what you believe. Strength grows by pushing through difficult situations and coming out on the other side feeling good about having done so. What you focus your attention on is what you are creating. It's a mental attitude, and that hopeful, mental attitude produces good brain chemicals. Resiliency will create your life story mentally and physically.

Horrible things happen in life, and there is no preventing them. Being miserable about something from long ago will completely disempower you. Focusing on the pain and negativity of the past will not change your story. The past is irrevocable; the present is a choice. Sometimes there are dark, heavy wounds that must heal; other times it's deep-seated negative thoughts and insecurities. Either way, the internal damage continues to exist due to lifelong habitual thoughts. For those heavy wounds, tell your story, get the support you need and let it go. Your view of difficult events coupled with your circle of support will determine your worldview. Relationships are influential and impacting your thought patterns. Creating a support system that helps you focus your attention on strength will assist in setting the tone of your mental health. Surround yourself with those with whom you can share your story, and who will help in pulling out the thread of optimism. Like a contagious virus, the microorganism of attitude is passed from one person to another. Unknowingly and unintentionally, painful life circumstances continue to define you, but realize that is a choice you are making daily with your thoughts and your surroundings. Your choices are interwoven with who you are on the inside.

Perhaps you haven't felt you were resilient in the past, but that does not mean you can't build it in the present. I can't say enough about the story you tell yourself. Your internal dialogue is with you all the time and resiliency or victimization is formed from that dialogue. Anger, hurt, depression, confusion, and defensiveness are all normal emotions, but let them work for you and not against you. Emotions exist so that we work through them and become the image of our best possible self. You have a right to all of your feelings; you also have a choice in how you wear them. A person's perception, be it true or false, is real inside the mind and body. That story has created you and will continue to create you until you change it. Your past story, if you are not careful will weigh you down and stifle your dreams. Your body and soul feel your story. Your happiness and peace of mind come from what continuously rolls around in your head.

Resiliency is built out of hopes, dreams, determination, willingness, and mental attitude. It is growing to have an optimistic heart. It's about learning to listen to that small, inner voice which will guide and comfort you if you give it a chance. The beautiful added perk to building resiliency is that it improves self-esteem. You gain confidence and strength in yourself and can feel good about who you are becoming. As you empower your own mind, you grow as an individual. Positive mental thinking is one of the most powerful tools on earth and gives you the potential to heal and release all past wounds. Feed your soul with good stuff, create an environment of hope, and pay attention to the story inside your head. Good emotional health is about being able to regulate your thoughts and emotions regardless of life circumstances. Resilience and optimism require effort and commitment on your part, but emotional happiness is the reward.

Chapter Six

The Spiritual Side of Darkness

"The wound is the place where light enters you." — Rumi

It's hard to imagine that there is a spiritual side of darkness. That pain, anger, disappointment, heartache or outright misery could be the place where light is found. When I speak of darkness, I am talking about the human flaw in all of us, the fractures in our spirit and the holes in our heart. There are times we experience pain so deeply that our thoughts take us to negative, nasty, unkind places. Sometimes people commit horrible, unkind acts which are incomprehensible, rendering us speechless. Natural disasters occur destroying our homes, our valuables and our security. And daily disappointments steal our joy. Tragedy and sorrow exist saturating the heart with emotions of darkness. It's up to us to find healthy ways to move through life's unpredictable changes.

Most of our awakening moments come from those places of darkness. Once while sitting with a client, hearing a troublesome story of abuse, my heart hurt in dreaded agony, when suddenly in my head I heard Louis Armstrong singing, "and I think to myself what a wonderful world." It felt genuine and true; tenderness and compassion washed over me. Distracted by my own thoughts, I was perplexed by what my heart was experiencing. Sitting in the face of agony, I felt "one" with my client and with the world around me. In that moment I saw darkness as nothing more than suffering for both the victim and perpetrator. Pain can bring out the worst in us, and if we can work through it, we discover our best. Judgment about pain gets in our way and clouds our thoughts with negative, nasty opinions. Once we do that, our hearts close and we too begin to feel contaminated inside.

This young woman was vulnerable, open and hopeful for a chance at healing. She wasn't blaming or hate-filled, just sad. In her pain I could see the gift—she was willing to stretch herself, to be uncomfortable, so that she could be different. She wanted to feel happier in her soul, to forgive, and to be a better, more available person and parent to her children. Pain is what made this woman break open, which in turn allowed me to be broken open; and so it goes.

The brain doesn't distinguish or prefer one emotion over another. It is as impartial as sitting at a stop light choosing to turn left versus right. Emotions are neither good nor bad. We have separated them, perhaps for the distinction of how to behave as a society—for example, patience is good, and anger is bad. Not only have we made the distinction between good and bad emotions, but we also deem some emotions appropriate or right and others wrong. Happiness, laughter, excitement, joy, and love are good emotions. Bad emotions are depression, fear, anxiety, anger, and defensiveness. Right emotions are forgiveness, compassion, honor and loyalty. Wrong emotions are lust, greed, envy, and hatred. Could it be possible to take a minute and honor all emotions as a necessary part of the building blocks that compose the heart and soul? The issue is not our wealth of amazing and scary emotions; the issue is how we have learned to express them.

After the book, *When Things Fall Apart* was released; I saw an interview with the author, Pema Chodron. The interviewer asked Pema why she used such a "depressing" title, insinuating it would create disinterest. As best as I can recall, Pema tenderly replied, "because things will fall apart." Those simple words took up residence in my thoughts. That is true—they fall apart, meet repair and fall apart again. The birth of resiliency, peace and happiness are followed by the learning curve of things falling apart and of us learning to pick up the pieces and put life back together again. Our culture has developed an insatiable need to avoid pain, loss and suffering. The avoidance of the inevitable is what makes the embracing of that thing so difficult. We are going to be disappointed, our hearts are going to be broken, fear is a must, anxiety is real, hatred is a reaction, and death a certainty.

Everything in Life Is About Transformation

Every known emotion will exist at some point in your life; there's no avoiding them, nor should you. The goal is to learn from the ones that are dark, so that you become more adept at moving through this unpredictable world. Darkness gives us the opportunity to be transformed, to be made better, wiser, and more compassionate. We shy away from failure and disappointment, assuming our weak egos cannot sustain the blow. When in reality, the best indicator of a strong ego is the ability to move through adversity. The desire to quickly rid oneself of a dark emotion is what causes them to be so jarring. The constant battle of denial and resistance creates continued unnecessary suffering. Until you become accepting of those difficult, dark places and allow them to move through you, they will leave you feeling overwhelmed and out of control until extinguishing them becomes an obsession.

We aren't taught how to sit with pain, how to sort through confusion or to take accountability for our part in our own suffering. Instead, we grasp at diversions such as television, the computer, alcohol, food and shopping to ease the discomfort. The mind can only do one thing at a time, so while you are distracted, the darkness doesn't feel present. Remember, stress and anxiety are cumulative. Your temporary distraction does not mean the distress goes away; it is simply stored in the body. There are gifts that come from dark emotions, and one of the best gifts of all is that you learn the skill of embracing the inevitable while becoming more enlightened. In reality, most have more good experiences than negatives; however, the pendulum will swing between light and the challenges of darkness. Navigating through difficult emotions is a skill that can be learned. True peace comes from balancing life as it rises and falls.

Many carry deep-seated insecurities and doubt which is derived more from self-esteem issues than from dark emotions, and this makes it difficult to sit with feelings. But don't think for a minute that insecurity and doubt are emotions that should be avoided. They too are a natural part of life. It is your seething, internal dialogue, jolted by what you believe about the insecurity that takes you down a path of emotional destruction. A low sense of self-esteem sends people into a whirlwind of murky emotions leading to defensiveness, followed by a flurry of dramatic negative self-talk. As a result, we have become so uncomfortable with dark emotions that we either avoid them at all costs or rip ourselves apart internally for having them.

Because of the inability to be with one emotion, work it through and let it dissipate, we wind up with a cascade of other overwhelming feelings. It's appropriate to feel weak, wrong, vulnerable and scared. Everyone feels those things more than you can imagine. When you internalize and judge yourself because of those unpleasant emotions, it fuels feelings of dread. Normalize them, bring them into the light for exposure and see yourself simply having a human experience. They pass; they don't last forever. Fighting with emotions, however, makes you feel worse on the inside and less able to deal with dark spaces when they come.

When suffering is present, the hyper-focus on misery creates more misery with downward spiraling thoughts. Deeper, darker thoughts can lead to horrible self-loathing judgment. It's necessary to feel discomfort when you are in it and to reach out and tell your story in an effort to gain the support you need. But pain, tainted with negativity, becomes a runaway train. It's easy to start thinking about dark emotions, feeding them with other negative thoughts, and then spewing them out to others. If not careful, one normal, dark emotion can create a dramatic story of negativity, and victimization becomes the focus. Few of us have been taught to sit with suffering as suffering and to trust the process. It's a natural inclination to want to feel good, but feeling good has become such the focus that it is attached to self-worth; so battling, blaming and denying dark emotions has become a way of life.

The misery connected to painful emotions confuses the mind and leaves the brain in a biochemical quandary. You're trying not to feel bad, yet all the while you are negatively focused on the not-so-good feelings. The brain of course just keeps producing chemicals based on your thinking. Your focus is negative, so the brain will eventually produce negative chemicals in response. What if the next time you get your feelings hurt, feel anxious or sad, you just took a few minutes and sat with those feelings? What if you didn't start pulling past wounds to the forefront of your brain and you didn't allow yourself to go into other types of negative thinking? What if, you simply sat with this one episode and said, "I feel really sad right now, but it's going to be okay. I got my feelings hurt, but I'm okay?" What if you took a deep breath and let your feelings sit in your soul with no chastising, storytelling, blaming or heaping on other emotions? What if you then released them and stopped clutching the pain so tightly? What if you choose not to focus on it? Painful emotions are part of our growth process. Learn to be with them, sit with them without judgment or drama, comfort your own soul, and honor your vulnerable humanness. You can't possibly be transformed without being cut open, and dark emotions will cut you wide open. However, darkness will rise, and it will dissipate if you will only create the space.

Darkness Can Illuminate the Soul

Everyone gets a turn. Hostility, heartbreak, grief, disappointment, betrayal, lust, greed and envy live in all. We want so badly to deny their presence as if denying them makes them somehow less real. Those distasteful emotions you think of as dark are what prompt you to look inside yourself for improvement. Believe it or not, they appear so that you may be awakened. They help you recognize when you have crossed an invisible line of your moral compass or abandoned your beliefs. They help you feel embarrassment, shame, humility, regret, remorse and tenderness. And when you feel these things, you are moved to pay attention and make improvements. They awaken compassion, move you toward forgiveness, and connect you as part of a community. Dark emotions make you work harder, appreciate the good in life, and can awaken you to a more soulful experience. Hard places touch the soul, and with tenderness will ease you closer to your best possible self. Not only do they help you look inside yourself for mistakes you may have made, they help you look to others for guidance, reassurance and forgiveness. If you believe you have over-disciplined your child, you will seek advice from a companion, family or friends. If you feel embarrassed in a situation, you may ask others if you were out of line; healthy input helps you self-regulate your behavior for future situations. When you have wronged someone, feelings of guilt prompt you to ask forgiveness.

As you learn to trust the dark emotions, you will see the gifts in doubt, anger, frustration and failure. The moment you experience failure, your brain begins trying to figure out what went wrong and how to rectify it, so the same mistake doesn't recur. The neurotransmitters in your brain are wired to problem-solve failure and work toward improvement. For example, if you lose your job, immediately you begin brainstorming how to become re-employed. Failure encourages you to work harder and think outside the box. Doubt will cause you to search. It allows the mind to question, which opens up pathways to options. Frustration is telling you to look inside yourself. It's a good motivator for a self-check, "am I over-reacting, fatigued, or do I need to take a break or walk away?" Anger lets you know that you have been wronged or treated unfairly. When someone is abusing you, anger can motivate you to get out of a bad situation. It will help you separate yourself from negative, damning people, or to take social action to create change. Shame can alert you to do a reality-check of your actions and perhaps change them, and envy can help you generate motivating goals. Yes, in the face of distress, some will fall into negative, self-defeating thoughts of helplessness, taking on the attitude of "woe is me." Falling prey to thoughts of victimization is learned from your environment and created from mind chatter.

We, as a species, are wired to survive and that survival is based on having dark emotions. Deep within the limbic system of the brain is the amygdala. Thought of as the "reptile or lizard brain," the amygdala is the primitive sector of the brain programmed for survival. It's the part of you that produces emotions, some of them dark, which make you respond and help you stay alive. The amygdala prepares the body for response, escape, and defense. Not only does it produce emotions, but it is also responsible for memory, and survival instincts. It stores things to memory, like a snake bite or the threat of a tiger, so that you remember and have that awareness for your future safety. It also stores to memory people and situations that have caused you harm, so that you can create a healthy distance between you and them. Somehow nature knew that we needed emotions to survive and thrive as a species, and we have a gland for that. You see, we think of our painful, reactive emotions as dark because they don't make us feel good and we want to feel good all of the time. But, those dark emotions are necessary. Anger, fear, suspicion, dread make us respond; it is our conditioning that has caused us to take emotions too far. There are things in life that need to be avoided. There are times when anger is appropriate. There are moments we should feel shame, regret and remorse. Our self-worth and self-preservation are achieved through awareness created from negative emotions. The trick is to become healthy enough to know when your emotions are on task or when they are way out of line.

Dark emotions move us to change. They help us gain insight and to have a stronger sense of consciousness. They help us individually and collectively as a community. Our survival instincts are not just for ourselves; we need one another for optimal living.

Emotions, good or bad, help us improve our individual life, and help form and manage the community at large. There would be social chaos were it not for dark emotions. Imagine the speeding, road rage, social outbursts, and public rudeness; not to mention the emotional upheavals that go on behind closed doors. The fear of getting a ticket keeps us from running red lights, and a healthy dose of guilt keeps us from taking things that don't belong to us. There are social mores that help keep behavior in check, and some of those are originally upheld due to avoidance of condemnation. One might question if that is a good system to have in place; live without it for a while and then ask that question.

Lawrence Kohlberg was a psychologist who studied moral development; meaning "how we develop right versus wrongdoing." To break it down into three groups, moral development looks something like this. Beginning in childhood, people evolve to do what's "right" or socially appropriate based on: 1- the avoidance of consequences, or the fear of punishment; 2 - the desire to be seen as good, the awareness of the observation of others; 3 - individual awareness and moral principles; right doing because in your heart you know it's the proper thing. As we grow, the hope is that we move toward the third level, the development of one's own sense of moral consciousness; even if we don't achieve it in every situation. Referring back to our earliest conditioning; we learn our actions, behaviors, values and attitudes from our environment, which is also where we learn to deal with dark emotions. We grow within ourselves and within our community because of uncomfortable emotions. Things bother you because sometimes, they are supposed to. Hard emotions keep you on your toes and help you expand your awareness. They make you stretch and want to become the hero that lives inside you. They develop wisdom; they make you work toward change, self-improvement and transformation in the world in which you live. Hard, painful emotions of outrage have established the most needed changes in our society. Changes in freedom, liberty and justice have come about because of disturbing hurt, angry feelings.

Feelings Demand Actions

With painful emotions, comes a call to action. Aching, longing and discomfort stir something inside us that, hopefully, will make us want to improve ourselves or our environment. We are moved to deliver glaring looks of shame, to confrontation and even reporting things we observe as publicly inappropriate. How quickly heads turn when a child is screaming, or perhaps being chastised in public. We not only want to keep ourselves in check, but we are also moved to keep those around us in check. As we grow into a sense of our own moral code, we notice when things around us don't seem quite right.

There has been a growing concern of social consciousness regarding abuses, poverty, and war, equal rights, taking care of the planet, fair trade, and global warming. This awareness often comes from disturbing images and information that make us feel pain. People go into cancer research because someone's mother or child died from the disease. Domestic violence projects, sustainable living environments, organic crop growing all exist because of tenderness we carry in our hearts. Action comes from emotional arousal. We are awakened to the reality of our individual and collaborative destructions because of feelings of guilt, shame, regret, fear, remorse, and sorrow. The countless number of clients who have come to my office with a lifetime of sadness, regret, anger, jealousy, depression and anxiety were motivated to change because of dark emotions. We change ourselves and our world because we feel the sting of darkness as it rises to our consciousness, and shows itself by causing us to suffer.

It's important to be patient, loving and kind with yourself as you learn and grow to higher stages of development and consciousness by making mistakes and being in dark places. Your higher development won't come to you automatically; it's achieved through being uncomfortable, through your morals and values being tested, through your heart being broken, and at times feeling as if your mind will explode. Dark emotions, all of them, serve a purpose. Their purpose is not to hurt you or make you have a miserable life. They are to provoke you into awareness and responsiveness. Apathy and complacency, for some, may be desired, at least temporarily, but apathy can soon feel like a life in hell. Nothingness is not a desirable state for human beings. We want to taste, touch, and feel. We desire hot tea, cold water, sweet ice cream and sour lemons. We long, laugh, ache, and ponder. Curiosity, fantasy and wonder are as much a part of us as the air we breathe. We can't help but want to feel alive, and part of feeling alive is the inevitable pendulum that will swing between light and darkness.

For life to change, grow or transition there must be growing pains. I believe with pure conviction in my heart that if you look deeply enough at any situation, there is a golden nugget and your life, somewhere and in some way, flourishes out of suffering. Allow the dark places to chisel out the best in you. If you can pause and allow consciousness to arise when dark emotions are present, they can teach you something about yourself, and they will teach you a higher level of consciousness about the world around you. They can create within you a richer more whole life.

Exercise: Touching the Dark Side

Everyone has moments of dark emotions. We try to minimize or avoid them because we are uncomfortable with the darkness and it causes us pain. However, the more we try to push dark emotions down, the more likely they are to surface and remind us that they are there. Remember dark emotions are part of the human experience and can help us grow in wisdom and strength.

- The next time you experience darkness, take a few moments and sit with that emotion. Focus on it so you can see what it's all about. Allow yourself to feel hurt or disappointed by whatever is going on.

- Ask yourself why you feel angry, resentful, negative or whatever. You may be angry that you did not get a job promotion, or feeling hurt by someone you love. Sometimes we may be in a dark space simply because we are having a bad day.

- Instead of focusing negative energy outward at other people and casting blame, look inward and ask yourself what role you play in the dark emotion. Maybe you hold back at work instead of being a go-getter, or maybe you have been guarded with your loved one and taking things personally.

- Ask yourself what change needs to occur with you or with your actions. For example, "I need to be more open and engaging. Or, I need to be less sensitive and judgmental."

- Write down three things you are willing to do differently around that dark emotion.

- Then offer a word of gratitude stating you are grateful for the darkness as it has made you aware so that now you can bring light into that dark space.

It is wise to visit emotions that disturb you; they are there to get your attention. If you look closely, you may learn some things about yourself that could change your life. Recognize it is your experience, and you are a contributing factor. As we look outward and blame the world, nothing will change. When we look inward, own our part in any situation, we create the potential for change. Darkness is present so that we may be awakened and create the light that we desire.

Chapter Seven

In Hot Pursuit of Happiness

"We aren't guaranteed Happiness, just the pursuit of it."
— Benjamin Franklin

Happiness is perhaps the most sought-after emotion on the planet. Each day we wake looking for that feeling, and even more importantly, spend our life trying to find ways to hang on to its essence once we have captured it. Elusive, happiness seems to get away from us as quickly as it comes; leaving us puzzled about how to create true joy in our daily lives. It's definitely the most discussed topic in therapy but relative to being unhappy. Through our desperate attempts to secure happy feelings, which we assume will alleviate suffering; we have become a materialistic and over-medicated society. Stress, frustration, heartache, loss, depression and anxiety create such feelings of emotional distress that we will do almost anything to loosen the grip. Dark emotions are avoided, and numbing efforts occur with attempts to rid the mind of obsessive and painful thoughts. Unfortunately, the things we are doing to feel better, in the long run, make us feel worse.

The aim of the pursuit of happiness is, in and of itself, happiness. Happiness is not tangible. You can't hold it in your hand, eat it, drink it, wear it, or drive it. These are things that make us feel comfortable and may momentarily boost our energy or esteem, but they have nothing to do with happiness. Even the end result of achieving your desire does not bring the craved feeling of final happiness. There is no final happiness. Our great joy is found in the journey and, unfortunately, we have lost sight of that fact. The thought, the momentum and excitement of an event or occurrence, is when the heart races. It's when our minds start dreaming and getting excited. Tenderness, kindness, the touch of a hand, a teardrop, true connection; those are moments of happiness. We can't help but desire, but once we achieve our heart's desire, the heart will desire yet again. Joy is found in the desire, not in the accumulation of the desired. Desire is what sparks possibility, ambition, and hope, but in our world of plenty, constant desire has set us up for unhealthy yearning.

The focus of desire, for most, centers on tangible items, or on comfort and ease. We are searching and assuming things outside of ourselves will create happiness and peace of mind. Indulgence and the achievement of comfort have made us less able to tolerate discomfort. With great comfort comes a loss of gratitude and humility. Too much comfort also creates the desire for more comfort. Like a drug, the more we have, the more we want. It's not the wanting that has created the dissonance, but the assumption that we should have all that our heart desires; that life should be easy and darkness should be evaded. As we have become inundated with the luxuries society has given, the beauty of simplicity is lost. To dream, to imagine, and to experience fantasy is what stimulates the heart.

Accepting disappointment and being able to bounce back creates a stronger sense of self than the self that is created out of having all that the mind wants.

Most never stop to think about the power we have over our own emotions, body, mind and true joy. You may presume you are helpless in creating desired outcomes, but you are capable of much more emotionally than you may know. Life won't always go your way, but happiness is always within your reach. The little things that make a happy heart are more often than not overlooked and made an insignificant part of your day. Internal discomfort has gradually been replaced with external, temporary pleasures. As the newness of those pleasures wears off, the discomfort returns, and we grasp externally yet again. To paraphrase the words of Mr. Spock, "After a time, you may find that having is not so pleasing as wanting."

I have seen the quest for happiness avalanche into a cascade of frustrating emotions that leave people debilitated by depression, anxiety, sleep disorders, eating disorders, relationship conflict, pain disorders, physical illness and disease. A constant yearning for external happiness and belief that you don't have it will make the mind and body ill. Happiness is not the problem; it's the belief of helplessness about unhappiness that causes internal instability. When you focus on unhappiness, unhappiness is what shows up, in the mind, the heart and in your reality. The heart can't help but long for happiness, but when the mind won't relinquish thoughts of unhappiness; eventually one or the other dominates—it's usually the mind. The mind holds your beliefs, habits, judgments, fears and insecurities; it's powerful beyond explanation.

Unhappiness is created out of your thoughts, and the acquiring of happiness is attempted through external measures. Those external measures work, but only temporarily. You can't trick the heart with pseudo-happiness; it knows the difference. A constant quest for happiness and beliefs focused on unhappiness will work your nerves, creating misery because the heart won't be silenced. The goal is to get the heart and mind working together; that's how you'll discover true happiness. Happiness is really about peace; a peace that can be present throughout our lives, even in times of death, sorrow, heartbreak and complete and utter disappointment.

The Heart and Soul of Happiness

Happiness is a soul journey. You don't turn it off and on; there's no beginning and end. It's not obtained, lost and obtained; although at times it may feel it has slipped away. Recognizing the moment, learning to be present in all moments even when they are painful, and knowing it will pass is the heart and soul of happiness. Happiness is gained through the ability to accept disappointments and heartaches, and seeing the gift that arises from those moments. It's about letting go of unnecessary burdens that labor around with you daily because you believe you must carry them. It's letting go of the past, not blaming others or expecting miracles…it's about making them. True happiness is intentional.

Happiness requires that you get still and go inward. Learn to make peace with life's disappointing moments. It doesn't mean that you won't get discouraged, feel great pain, anger, or outrage. It means you settle into your heart and soul on how to move through those things. Part of happiness is enjoying good food, great laughter, bursts of energy that comes with dreaming, success, or accomplishment. But most importantly, it's about learning not to expect to live in those places. Happiness is a feeling that comes from the soul and is felt right down to the core of your existence. And it is awakened by the little things, the big things, the insignificant moments, and the ones you miss because of your mistaken image of happiness.

We are enamored by those who have the courage to walk away from their prescribed life in search of happiness—the *Reader's Digest* version of stories about those who leave their large homes, high-stress jobs, or crowded cities build hopes and dreams for all. Vicariously you are touched as you read the stories; their bold choices tap into dreams of your own. There is a belief that if you can just get away from your overwhelming life, happiness will be yours. It's not to say that it doesn't happen, that leaving a job, a city or unbearable stress can change a life. It's not the leaving; it's the mindset. The learned belief gets stuck on bigger, more, and better. Yet, the more you acquire, the busier and more complex life becomes and all the while, you desire a simpler life. And why do you think that is so? Because deep in every heart, there is a knowing that simpler is more peaceful, the little things are more joyous, and in still moments you can feel true happiness. There is a beautiful essay by Robert Hastings, which sums up the ability to know lasting happiness.

The Station

Tucked away in our subconscious minds is an idyllic vision. We see ourselves on a long, long trip that almost spans the continent. We're traveling by passenger train, and out the windows we drink in the passing scene of cars on nearby highways, of children waving at a crossing, of cattle grazing on a distant hillside, of smoke pouring from a power plant, of row upon row of corn and wheat, of flatlands and valleys, of mountains and rolling hillsides, of city skylines and village halls, of biting winter and blazing summer and cavorting spring and docile fall.

But uppermost in our minds is the final destination. On a certain day at a certain hour, we will pull into the station. There will be bands playing and flags waving. And once we get there, so many wonderful dreams will come true. So many wishes will be fulfilled, and so many pieces of our lives finally will be neatly fitted together like a completed jigsaw puzzle. How restlessly we pace the aisles, damning the minutes for loitering, waiting, waiting, waiting for the station.

However, sooner or later we must realize there is no one station, no one place to arrive at once and for all. The true joy of life is the trip. The station is only a dream. It constantly outdistances us. When we get to the station that will be it! We cry, "When I'm eighteen that will be it! When I buy a new 450 SL Mercedes Benz that will be it! When I put the last kid through college that will be it! When I have paid off the mortgage that will be it! When I win a promotion that will be it! When I reach the age of retirement that will be it! I shall live happily ever after!"

Unfortunately, once we get "it" then "it" disappears. The station somehow hides itself at the end of an endless track. "Relish the moment" is a good motto. It isn't the burdens of today that drive men mad. Rather, it is regret over yesterday or fear of tomorrow. Regret and fear are twin thieves who would rob us of today. So, stop pacing the aisles, and counting the miles. Instead, climb more mountains, eat more ice cream, go barefoot more often, swim more rivers, watch more sunsets, laugh more and cry less. Life must be lived as we go along. The station will come soon enough.

You have been conditioned to believe that "if or when" you reach a certain place in life, you will then find happiness. One temporary fix leads to another, each time setting you up for more disappointment. The problem is as you live for "when" and chase something outside of yourself there will not be enough, and you will feel the recurring agony of defeat. That interpretation of desire and defeat reduces your ability to enjoy right now. Happiness is inside you; desire gives the mind options to ponder. But when desire becomes equated with fulfillment and failure, the purpose of desire and happiness are lost.

The ability to pick yourself up and dust yourself off when darkness prevails will determine your level of happiness. People who create happiness from within tend to be more internally motivated or proactive leading to positive outcomes. Remember, what you focus your attention on is what you draw to you. Happy people produce happy results, which sometimes looks and feels like the treasures of external happiness. But those treasures are accomplished by their ability to keep moving forward no matter what. They do tend to reach their goals more often than those who carry thoughts of unhappiness and doubt within. Not necessarily because they are fortunate, or lucky, but because they have acquired the capability to be in hard, dark moments and to keep moving forward.

The Power of Grief

I worked with a woman who came to therapy following the loss of her mother. She was experiencing confusion because of feelings of apathy in her life. Seventeen months earlier, her mother passed away which was a staggering loss in Carol's life. She had been extremely close to her mother and was her caretaker until the time of her death. Carol, an only child, was in her mid-twenties when her father died, which built an even closer relationship between her and her mother. Carol sought therapy because she thought "maybe" she was depressed or "something was wrong because she felt nothing and she just wasn't herself."

Carol described herself as having a good life with her husband and children and thought she had a great relationship with her mother. During her mother's three-year battle with cancer, Carol had been distraught with grief but admitted her emotions were dominated with focusing on hope and being present in her mother's life. Carol's concern was that since her mother's death, she had never actually cried, she didn't think of her very often, and recently had not even thought about her mother on her birthday. Confused by her emotions, Carol wondered if maybe she wasn't as close to her mother as she had previously thought as she seemed to carry no tenderness in her heart.

"Sometimes I hold my mother's picture in my hands and stare at it for a really long time trying to feel something inside. I want to cry; I want to feel sad. I want to miss her, but I don't. I just don't. I do in my mind, but I don't in my heart. I feel like I'm looking at a stranger. Then when I missed her birthday, I knew something was wrong with me. I know I was close to mom my entire life, she was my confidant, my friend and the thought of her dying really was devastating to me. Then she passes away and nothing? The months click by and nothing? It's as if she and her memory vanished from my life. I know it sounds crazy, but I'm numb and miserable because I'm numb. Not sad, not hurt, not brokenhearted, but miserable maybe because I feel empty."

Carol shared glimpses of the life she shared with her mother, even brought in pictures from time to time so I could know her. There were great stories. There was a history of tenderness and closeness, joy and connection. I could see why she wanted to feel her stories and why she wanted to grieve the loss of a person so dear to her heart. Carol was a warm and soulful person but was detached from her emotions. One of the things I learned while getting to know

Carol was that once they knew her mother was not going to survive, friends and family suggested Carol go on an antidepressant as losing her mother would be too overwhelming for her to handle. This stood out in my mind because it seemed to be the point at which she shut down and became removed from her emotions. When I discussed this with Carol, she admitted to concerns of being on medication but assumed she needed it and was too anxious to stop taking it.

For some, one of the side effects of antidepressants is apathy. And the problem with apathy is that often you don't feel enough even to know that you need to do something differently. There are many who believe that strong emotions are to be avoided and antidepressants are appropriate in times of great sorrow. While that is an individual decision, it is not a decision that should be taken lightly. There is often great confusion about suffering versus depression. Quickly our society jumps to the conclusion that suffering, heartbreak and loss are synonymous with a clinical diagnosis of depression. There is a very notable difference. Anyone can become vulnerable to the pain of out of control emotions, and a lack of knowing how to move through them which can result in the use of medications.

When we love someone, we don't want to see them in pain; we want their suffering to abate. When we are devastated and heartbroken, we want our pain to subside. Medications can, and do, shut off some of the brain receptors so that there are fewer emotional transmitters occurring. The problem that arises when emotions are shut down is that emotions are shut down. You don't get to pick and choose between the good and bad ones. While many do want painful emotions to simply go away; there is a loss of self when closed off from suffering. Self is created out of all emotions, the good and the bad. The avoidance of pain is not healthy and even detrimental to anyone's mental health, and the soul knows it.

The soul doesn't shy away from suffering; it is capable of being in the heart of all. Programmed thinking and beliefs about yourself convince you that you cannot be in the heart of suffering. Because of this, it becomes difficult to see the gift and growth in heartaches. There is a Japanese form of pottery repair called Kintsukuroi. The translation means golden repair. Its origin says that when a piece of pottery is broken it is diligently put back together with lacquer and powdered gold and it becomes more beautiful for having been broken. The lines and cracks stand out and are noticeable. The breakage and the repair elevate the object to a higher level; for the time and patience it took to form its original creation, and then for the dedication to the repair. The fracture, instead of diminishing the value, deepens it with honor and respect. The object is also considered stronger following repair.

The first time I saw a pottery bowl repaired through Kintsukuroi, its beauty stopped me in my tracks. While at the home of one of my teachers it sat on a shelf and was more noticeable than anything else in the room. Being curious, and assuming it was originally constructed with the gold lines as part of its design, I asked about the piece of art. My teacher knowingly smiled, and that was the focal point of our lesson for the evening.

Hard places, when repaired, create the best in us. Those who have walked through the greatest darkness, shine with the brightest light. Suffering taps into the vulnerable heart, creates compassion and evolves the self. When we take the time to experience heartache and allow ourselves to grow, we develop greater strength than we had before. To feel and truly experience loss, to know disappointment and sorrow will teach us to be better within ourselves and with the world around us.

It's not easy to sit with suffering because once it is present, we become consumed with negative emotions of anger, resentment, bitterness, guardedness, and fear. The focus becomes about the fear of out of control emotions. But, if you can gain the courage to be with your dark emotion, you will develop emotional muscle and soulful living. Learn to stay present with the pain that exists not giving way to the maddening story that lives in your head. Grow to become self-soothing, knowing this will pass and you will be all right. Let it move through you and then slip away in tenderness. In so doing, you develop a greater respect for life, more tenderness toward others, stronger coping skills, and deeply satisfying relationships. Much like the repair of Kintsukuroi, we have greater value than before the breakage.

With the assistance of her doctor, Carol decreased and eventually ceased the use of antidepressants, and then the floodgates of grief were open. Her therapy was about learning to be in the agony of all that is real. She had to accept with pain and heartbreak that her mother was no longer on this earth. She had to accept that her friend and "go to" person was a memory to share, and grieve, and mourn. Carol told stories and relived many moments of her life with her mother. At times she wept passionately, so much that it was painful to sit across the room with the volume of her tears. The pain was breathtaking, and her healing profound. Carol grew, her physical and emotional appearance transformed before my eyes. She laughed more often, was radiant, lighter even in her tears and she beamed with a heart of golden streaks. Her grief made her a wiser, deeper, more beautiful and spiritual person.

The Strength of a Thousand Golden Strands

Our emotions connect us to the deepest and highest sense of self. They are what awaken us to the things that matter, and at times it must be through suffering. Your belief about yourself or your capabilities arises from your inner voice, and your inner voice comes from your internal emotional make-up. Captivated by quick and easy solutions, we assume the heart can't handle the pain that life requires of us. We lack the confidence needed to move through dark spaces and instead, look for an easy out. If you believe you cannot do a thing—you cannot do a thing. However, you'd be surprised what the heart and soul can handle. Each heartache that you consciously move through creates a golden strand that prepares you for the next.

We absolutely want and deserve to be happy. Through the years as a therapist, and in my own personal life, I have sought out and tried many worldly pleasures in trying to produce the proverbial peace and happiness we often hear about. There is something within us that believes there is a type of happiness that will keep suffering away. I believe it is unrealistic that anyone could have a life free from suffering, filled with ecstatic happiness all the time; however, there is a big difference between giddy happy and peaceful happy. The life we have will ebb and flow allowing us to feel the beauty of the highs when they are present, and hopefully, learn from the lows. Unknowingly, many live in angst and fear which will keep them from knowing the happiness that can be found inside of suffering. There is joy in grieving the loss of those dear to us. Happiness and confidence can be found in taking steps forward to move through job loss, divorce, or hardship. It is esteem building to work through tragedy, to hold hope in difficult moments, and to believe you can move through whatever life sets before you. Strength in yourself creates happiness within.

Each time you move through a difficult situation, a single thread is woven into your heart and brain. As the heart grows stronger, so does the wiring in the brain. And with the next heartache or disappointment, another golden stand is formed, and the next and the next. The brain and heart are being rewired by your ability to not only sit with difficulty but to grow from having the experience. Your weakness is perpetuated by your beliefs. Pain cannot be avoided and does not have to be seen as devastating and horrible. If you change your thoughts about suffering, you will change how you move through the inevitable. The strands of your life are woven together to form the tapestry of who you are. Your soul is being constructed one golden strand at a time, and you get to choose your tapestry of life. If you consciously choose to see joy, you will create a world of joy around you.

You don't have to pursue happiness—it's everywhere—you just have to choose to see it. Laughter and fun, good food and easy times will automatically show up in life, but so will heartache. Happiness is all of those things woven into the creation of who you are constantly becoming. Happiness is in holding the hand of a loved one as they leave this life. It's sitting at the side of a friend that's undergoing surgery or chemotherapy. Happiness is hearing the sobs of someone you care about whose heart has been split wide open. It can be saying goodbye to a marriage that is no longer filled with life or letting go of things that rob you of your joy. Happiness is paying attention; it is the willingness to be present in all of your life, and the ability to suffer when it's your time. Happiness is having faith in yourself and the world around you. It's a soul journey, but you have to be willing to go there. It's embracing the idea that everything in life is but a moment, and this too shall pass. Happiness is the strength of a thousand golden strands that you have earned while on your journey.

Chapter Eight

Five Steps to Rewiring Your Heart

"Success is the sum of small efforts, repeated day in and day out." — Robert Collier

Happiness, peace of mind, wisdom of heart, and passion of soul are fluid, will rise and fall, but are always available to you. You can, however, become more capable of consistently tapping into those things, if you take the steps to rework your prior wiring and conditioning. Change takes time and effort. The process through which you have become who you are was a slow ongoing process that you unconsciously took part in. With the right information, you have the potential to create the life and experience you desire consciously. The best and most productive path to enhance your own change is to appeal to the tenderness of your heart. We are emotional creatures; to honor that you deserve true joy, and that it can be accomplished, touches the emotional center of your being.

It starts with the human brain, which is astounding because it touches every single part of our existence. The brain communicates with and makes every minute part of your body functional. It alerts you to danger, causes you to long and desire, helps you remember, causes you to forget, motivates you, lulls you to sleep, helps you fall in and out of love, taps into your heart and makes you feel alive. And it even reaches the soul for higher levels of consciousness.

The brain is divided into two separate hemispheres; one being the logical, left brain and the other being the creative, right brain. Together and separate they each are responsible for making us whole but have very unique and specific purposes. The logical brain thinks in terms of details, past information and future planning. It is responsible for analyzing, judging, and reasoning. It is the intellectual voice that helps make sense of the world around us. The right brain is the creative, imaginative, intuitive part. It thinks in terms of the present moment, how things look, feel, sound and taste. It experiences the energy of life, through feelings and connection. The beauty of you, your brain, and your soul is that you can choose how you experience your life. You have the power to move back and forth between the two hemispheres of your brain. There are times you need your logic and reasoning, but there are times you need the emotions of heart and soul. You can create a mind and a brain that will work for you and with you so that your life experience is what you desire.

With awe and admiration, Jill Bolte Taylor springs to mind when I think of the power we have within. She is a brain scientist, who at the age of thirty-seven had a stroke, followed by the removal of a tumor in the left hemisphere of her brain, and a recovery that was phenomenal. She lost the ability to walk, talk, read or recall any of her life, and all the while remained in touch with her right brain, her emotional core. While having the stroke, she could see the power of her right brain at work creating beauty, passion and love. Dr. Taylor is a stunning example of determination, brain recovery potential, heart and soul. Following an eight-year journey of rehabilitation, she did recover, and in her book, *A Stroke of Insight* she describes her awakened experience.

"I felt enormous and expansive, like a genie just liberated from her bottle. And my spirit soared free like a great whale gliding through a sea of silent euphoria. Nirvana – I found Nirvana. There's no way I would ever be able to squeeze the enormousness of myself back inside this tiny little body. But then I realized I'm still alive. I'm still alive, and I have found Nirvana. And if I have found Nirvana and I'm still alive, then everyone who is alive can find Nirvana. And I pictured a world filled with beautiful, peaceful, compassionate, loving people who knew that they could come to this space at any time. And they could purposely choose to step to the right of their left hemispheres and find this peace. And then I realized what a tremendous gift this experience could be. What a stroke of insight this could be to how we live our lives. And it motivated me to recover..."

"...Who are we? We are the life-force power of the universe with manual dexterity and two cognitive minds. And we have the power to choose moment by moment who and how we want to be in the world. Right here, right now I can step into the consciousness of my right hemisphere where we are, I am the life-force power of the universe. I am the life-force power of the fifty trillion beautiful molecular geniuses that make up my form—at one with all that is."

We have the capability to move beyond our previous ways of thinking and the conditioning of our pasts to improve and empower the body and brain's functioning. There are great capacities for living in the emotional brilliance of the right brain, so that we may bring forth a knowing of what we need to be our best selves. Through the knowledge of science and the heart of therapy, we now know what has created who we are and how to transform what we have been taught. Therapy and science fit together beautifully. Therapy is the treatment of disease or disorder through rehabilitation or curative powers. Science is systematic knowledge gained through observation or experience. In the world of mental health, there is a combination of left brain and right brain efforts to rehabilitate the individual through the curative emotional process while paying very close attention to the client's experiences through observation and information. Science has put a great deal of effort into understanding the biology of the brain; psychotherapy puts enormous efforts into understanding human behavior as produced by the brain.

Therapy and science can come together to create some of the most powerful, psychological healing in our history. Through the understanding of neuroplasticity (the brain's ability to change and adapt), and consciously putting forth an effort to make changes, your emotional and physical health will transform. Your environment and behaviors of the past wired who you became; your actions and choices from this point forward can be rewired to create the person you desire. The following five steps are actions you can take to improve your health, happiness, relationships with self and other, and will help you find internal peace.

Five Stages to Rewiring your Heart

1. Exercise

Being able to move your body is a gift, and your body wants and needs to move. We are forces of energy, and when you are moving your body, you are stimulating the energy of body and mind. The simple force of external movement creates powerful forces of internal movement. Everything within you—from your heart, brain, blood, cells, joints and organs, right down to the thoughts you are thinking—are affected by the movement of your body. Exercise is not about losing weight or having a beautiful body; it's about feeling good in your body. Just moving that miraculous body for twenty minutes a day enhances mood stabilization, energy, brain responsiveness, and reduces your chances of heart attack, high blood pressure, cholesterol, and boosts your autoimmune system.

Agree to start. Take a walk every other day. Do an at-home workout video, go on a hike; take a bike ride, dance—just as long as you physically move your body. Exercise is the single best thing you can do for your brain as it generates positive electrical firing from within the brains cells, and it will reduce stress and anxiety, lift depression, increase energy, and improve mood and memory because it releases many positive brain chemicals.

2. Meditation

Meditation is a method of connecting the body, mind and soul. It quiets the mind, allows you and your body to sit in a place of serenity without judgment. It transcends the chatter of everyday life and allows your emotions to be removed from tension and stress. It opens up channels of peace and tranquility that awaken healing properties in your brain and taps into the soul of who you really are. Meditation creates relaxation in the body that is healing right down to a cellular level. Just the moments of peace felt within are invigorating. It creates a deeper connection with self and allows for deeper connection with others. Few things in today's world can calm and slow the angst within the body and brain as will the practice of meditation.

I recognize meditation can feel daunting, like something that is impossible to do or to do well. Because it isn't part of our background or culture, most think there is a "right" way to meditate. In one of my classes a woman desperate, but with laughter, said, "I don't know how to get my mind to go blank, so I don't think I'll ever be able to meditate." It's not about having a blank slate of mind; it's having a calming experience of mind and body. It's about relaxing the mind and transforming the multitude of busy thoughts. It is as simple as focusing on the gentleness of your breathing. When your subconscious mind begins to experience thoughts, gently guide your mind back to the attention of your breathing. You can also focus on a beautiful light, the beat of your heart or on radiating waves of kindness. The purpose is to create stillness, peace within the body and gentleness of your entire being. It isn't possible to have the mind go blank; it is possible to have the mind be still.

Learn to meditate, even if you don't feel you are good at it, persist. Brain research has proven that meditating a few times a week reduces negativity in the mind, enhances memory, feelings of hope, compassion, calmness and clarity. It improves creativity and daily productivity. Meditation creates structural changes in the brain connected with the body's ability to heal itself; it calms the amygdala (the emotional fight-flight center), decreases fear and anxiety, enhances sleep and improves depression.

3. Mindfulness

Some days you are probably more aware than others of how repetitive and intrusive your thoughts are. Without mindfulness, the mind is constantly moving from the past to future, with judgments, demands, expectations, needs, and failures. You're bombarded with thoughts, trying to remember what you forgot, where you need to be, what you should be doing, what you are feeling, what hurts you— the list is endless. These runaway thoughts cause emotional stress, fear and anxiety in the mind and body, and they steal your joy.

Mindfulness will help you learn to be in the moment and enjoy simple pleasures. It's achieved through becoming aware; learning to pay attention. Mindfulness creates consciousness, calms the body and soothes the heart. It allows you to notice, and then to choose your thoughts. If you are aware, mindfulness can keep you from brooding when you're upset. It can stop you from going off with anxious, negative, emotional chatter. It gives you the power to let go of those unwanted invasive thoughts. Studies show the practice of mindfulness reduces blood pressure, aids in the body's natural healing properties, improves sleep, memory, concentration, mental clarity, symptoms of depression and anxiety and promotes feelings of kindness and peace.

The next time you are having disturbing thoughts, create mindfulness by changing the channel. Notice your distracting thought and what it is doing to you, and then choose to let it go. Then, simply think about something else, carefully choose a different thought. If you are driving down the road thinking about work stress, take a deep breath and choose a thought of gratitude. Humble yourself and become grateful for the car you are driving, the hum of its engine, the arms that maneuver the steering wheel, or the eyes that see. Or, look out your window and notice a beautiful tree, a raindrop, or a peaceful sky. When your mind starts to wander, bring it back to a thought of choice. You can choose a pleasant thought to replace an unpleasant thought at any time. Thoughts are choices.

Mindfulness can awaken you to the consciousness of your life, allowing passion and tenderness to move through you simply because you are alive. It softens the heart, allows it to blossom with compassion, and naturally creates forgiveness within your soul. It is a spiritual practice, the art of intentional living. And it can do all of these things because your runaway thoughts are what creates madness, and dis-ease in the body, heart and soul.

4. Expand, Experience, Exposure

You and your brain are never too old to grow and learn. The old saying, "You can't teach an old dog new tricks" just isn't true. As we age, we become less active and less involved. It's easy to get into a routine and have that become your life. However, your surroundings, your daily choices and activities are constantly forming who you are, even as you age. Your experiences and exposures are forming the cell pathways and behavior of your brain with what you are taking in from the outer world. Your brain is modeling itself with imprints from the external stimuli of your exposure. As you get older, you may say, "been there and done that" but keep going and doing things. We are products of our environment.

Bring newness into your thinking; take in new ideas, information, or knowledge through exposure and experiences. Anything new or challenging expands the mind and ignites the neurons in your brain. Environment plays a vital role in health and activity of your brain. New stimuli and experience increases blood flow in your brain's cortex and neurons, and your cells will actually light up and produce positive firing. Healthy, new experiences allow you and your brain to keep growing.

Experiences and exposure can be anything from learning a new language, yoga, art, or tennis, to making pottery, playing a musical instrument, having a new conversation or reading a new book. New information challenges your brain by calling for it to be alert and attentive. It awakens the mind. When you expose yourself to a new class or group, it challenges your thinking. You expand by reading new material, taking part in a book club, volunteering, or doing any new and active event. Go to therapy or get involved in a group setting where you can be challenged or learn something about yourself. Read a self-help or spiritual book; take on an expanded way of thinking. Environment, information and activity are major factors in your brain and psychological health.

5. Mental Attitude

All of the above techniques will improve your mental attitude; however, you can make a conscious choice about the daily attitude of your life. There is an enormous energy behind the attitude that propels outcomes. Attitude is a way of thinking, and your way of thinking will construct your life.

Your attitude about an experience or life event will affect you more than the experience itself. You are your thoughts, and your brain will create misery or happiness, drama or serenity out of your thinking. A single thought can and will dictate the emotion that follows. You cannot have an emotion without first having a thought. Your attitude is not the emotion; it is the thought that triggers the emotion. Seriously, if you change your thoughts, you will change your life. It's just as easy to have good positive thoughts as it is to have harsh, negative thoughts, and your attitude determines which it will be.

With one thought after another, you are paving the emotional outcome of your life. You are either creating joy or the lack of joy in your being. If you have negative or harsh ways of thinking, you are consistently reinforcing an attitude—whether you are aware of it or not. What you think again and again or hold as true in your mind is what gets mapped in the brain. It's a practice, a practice in thinking. Mental attitude can be transformed with time and patience. Your brain and thoughts have developed over time, and it will take time and practice to develop new ways of thinking.

If you are willing to change your mental attitude, begin by drawing from the positives in your life. Go to sleep each night thinking of three good things that happened to you that day; wake each morning and acknowledge three gifts in your life. Even if you are struggling, there are gifts of gratitude in your world. Running water, lights, food and small acts of kindness are gifts. Humble yourself so you can see the little joys you are missing. Take gossip, criticism, and judgment out of your words and thoughts. Choose to take the negative impulses out of your life; they hurt you more than they hurt others. Reach out to people who will see the best in you. If you want a compliment, give a compliment. If you need a hug, give a hug. Don't wait for the joys of life to come to you, go to them.

Attitude is the most powerful tool you possess. It determines how you feel about yourself, others and the experience of your life. Your attitude can be your best friend or your worst enemy; it's up to you. A good attitude will develop resiliency in you, making your approach to the difficult moments in this life a little easier. "Attitude is a little thing that makes a big difference" (Winston Churchill). Don't underestimate the power of attitude, it can take the simplest problem and turn it into a crisis, and it can take a crisis and turn it into a challenge.

The Transformation of Marie

Years ago, I worked with a woman in her forties who suffered from symptoms of depression. Marie stated she didn't understand why but she was never "really happy" and felt bad more days than not. Her job was stable and not extremely stressful; there were no financial issues, marital issues, or family conflicts to speak of. She complained of low energy, lethargic feelings, sleeping too much, some slow but consistent weight gain. She admitted to isolating herself with the television and computer, stating she never felt like doing anything. Marie emphatically believed she had suffered from low-grade depression for years declaring that her mother suffered from depression and that it ran in her family.

I conceded that she was exhibiting symptoms of depression and suggested there were things she could do in her life to alleviate those symptoms. The first thing I recommended was that she incorporated exercise into her daily life. Marie insisted she didn't like going to the gym, "workout tapes are boring," and didn't want to exercise outside because she hated the heat and sweating. There was nothing I could say or do to get her to understand the positive effects of exercise for her body and mental health. We then discussed food, meditation, and community involvement, all of which she negated for one reason or another. Exasperated with me, she insisted her depression was genetic, and that was that.

By the time our next appointment rolled around, Marie had seen a doctor who concurred that she was suffering from depression and placed her on an antidepressant. Absolved, Marie was pleased, believing that she would now feel better and enjoy her life. She desperately wanted the medication to be the answer; however, over the next nine months, her therapy time was focused on the miseries of her medication. The first SSRI made her feel lightheaded as if she was going to faint, the second gave her raging headaches, the third caused sleeplessness which was addressed by her taking another medication.

As time passed, Marie didn't feel as well as she had hoped, and now there were a whole new set of complaints that she continued to contribute to her depression "getting worse." She no longer enjoyed sexual activity, she felt hung over in the mornings, gained more weight, and complained of being even more exhausted. Her doctor, in helplessness and not knowing what else to do, put Marie on one of the "add-on" drugs to help boost her antidepressant. Now she was on three medications. Within weeks she was crying almost daily; she denied having suicidal thoughts, but stated, "I wouldn't care if my car slammed into a tree and I wasn't here anymore." Within months I observed a woman with very minor depressive symptoms which could have been remedied with lifestyle changes, catapult into a full-blown depression.

Marie's decline continued, she took time off work and grew deeper and darker into sadness and isolation. As she got close to rock bottom, she decided to go off the medications because the side effects were too much for her to handle. Marie remained in therapy and became willing to do some personal work. We had a strong enough relationship now that she was willing to trust some of my therapeutic tactics which she had previously declined. I agreed to her request that we take easy slow steps as she stated she already felt horrible and defeated. We began by writing a daily, weekly and monthly motivation chart to help get her started.

The first thing I asked of Marie was that each morning she writes down three things for which she was grateful, and she did. Then I asked that before she closed her eyes each night, she would state three good things she encountered that day. We did this for two weeks and then added that she take a walk each day. This was more challenging. In trying to motivate her to walk daily, I decided to use gratitude and attitude to nudge her forward. As she complained, I asked that she visualize the numerous people in nursing homes, hospitals, or injured that would give anything to be able to walk around the block. And, I asked that before each walk she state, "I am grateful for my legs, my health and my freedom. I am grateful that I can walk this block, that I have hope and that I will get better." Marie's complaining decreased, and the amount of time she spent walking increased. Next, I asked that once every other week she engaged in any activity. The activity could be lunch with a friend, going to a play, volunteering, or going to talks or concerts at a local university. Then once a month, I started assigning her books to read that we would discuss in therapy. I desperately tried to get her to meditate, but that was the thing she could not embrace, so I let that one go.

Every other week at our appointment, I noticed improvements. There were sessions when we laughed and cut up, and times she was emotional and tender. Thankfully there were fewer and fewer signs of depression. Within a year, Marie was a transformed person. Her life routine was something I became utterly impressed with after having seen where she had been. Each morning she would read a few pages from a book, and write out three things in life for which she was grateful. Every afternoon she took a brisk walk around her neighborhood and even incorporated other physical activities when time permitted. She got involved in several monthly activities including a spiritual book club. Marie decided that each year she would take a new class, explore a new place or learn something new to add to her life skills. Marie kept the daily, weekly and monthly motivational chart we had made posted on the side of her fridge. She slept well, lost weight, laughed often and embraced, without fear and stress, moments of natural depressive symptoms she encountered. We jokingly called her my poster child for therapy.

The Power to Change

You are who you are because of the choices you make. The circuitries of your heart and brain have been trained, emotionally and physiologically through the repetition of your life. It is human nature to want something outside of ourselves to make things better, but realize that the design of your life is in your hands. You have the power to impact the biochemicals of your body and brain, and they will, and do, impact your mental health. Choosing to get up every day and make a difference in your own life; that is healing, that is powerful. Looking outside of yourself will only prolong the process and exhaust the mind and body. There are no instantaneous quick fixes; you're worth the journey. View the five stages to rewiring your heart as a gift, a gift to you. This is something you can do for yourself that will make you feel more alive. In choosing these five steps as conscious ways of living, you will rewire your thinking, your brain and your way of being in your body and in your soul.

There is an energy that we all live in each and every day of our lives, and that energy is manifested out of what we do or do not do. As you make these neural changes, you also change the vibrations of your body, mind and soul. These changes give you an opportunity for a different, more alive way to be on this earth. As energy within you moves or vibrates with a healthier sense of being, you open your heart to a more emotional and soulful way of life. One of my "isms" that I try to accept and live by is, "Everything in my life is a direct result of my own actions or inactions."

Chapter Nine

The Choices We Make, The Life We Create

*"It is our choices, Harry, that show what we truly are, far
more than our abilities." — JK Rowling*

You are formed of energy. And the energy of your thoughts is the
momentum of your life. It powers what you do, your relationships,
what you believe about yourself, and what others see in you. All of
life is constructed of energy. The universe, this planet, your cell
body all work in perfect balance because of a constant flowing
energy. How miraculous and beautiful. Thoughts and emotions
coexist because of something called vibrational energy. Your
vibrational energy is your overall state of being. If you are not
getting enough sleep, if you are not eating well, or are filled with
fear, doubt and insecurity, you are vibrating at lower levels. When
you are feeling well, laughing, exercising, or having good thoughts,
you are producing energy that is vibrating at higher levels.

You are constantly drawing life to you whether it is in the form
of happiness, creativity, and hope or negativity, hopelessness and
resentment. Your internal energy always begins with your thinking,
and eventually, you will breathe life into those thoughts with your
behavior or attitude. Energy is recognizable; you can see and feel it
in others, and you can see and feel it in yourself. And it works hand

and hand with the law of attraction—like attracts like. You draw to yourself based on what you are experiencing internally.

We think in terms of vibes coming and going from one person to another, but seldom stop and think about what that really means. Vibes are the movement of emotional energy that is being transmitted and received. We feel each other through energy. Energy can be anything from thoughts to words, actions and attitude. Vibes are a smile, scowl, a handshake, hurriedness, hesitation or an embrace. You are generating vibes inside your body, sending those out into the world and receiving vibes from other sources. You are making a statement to everyone around you with your vibes. And your vibes are affecting you in one way or another. Should you desire changes in your life, you must choose to vibrate at a different level.

Vibrations motivate us, draw things to us, and communicate with others about us. They allow us to feel and experience ourselves and our environment. They transport the love and beauty of this life into our consciousness. The tenderness of children and puppies, the joys in snowfalls and sunny days, the grief and sorrow of losing a loved one, compassion for world tragedies, and heartbreaks that bring us to our knees exist because of vibrational energy. These would be nothing more than passing events were it not for energy vibrating inside us. Our vibrations allow us to feel authentically alive or emotionally depleted. And we are creating the energy of our lives.

Imagine that you have an electromagnetic field in the form of a bubble that surrounds you and extends five to ten feet in circumference. Inside the circle is your energy source and you are creating the energy within. As you and your bubble move around in your environment, you are moving energy out in front of you as you go. You will touch people with your energy field, you will consciously and subconsciously draw people into your circle, and you will bump into others in public areas. Your engagements will be determined by the force and type of your energy because only like energies want to share the same space. Some will reject or engage with your energy based on who they are in conjunction with who you are. Likewise, you will reject or connect based on your interpretation of other energy vessels. You are the keeper of your emotional internal electromagnetic energy, you decide what energy lives inside your circle, and you decide what incoming energy permeates your space. You can decide it consciously or unconsciously, but you are the determining factor.

What is the Energy of your Life?

Creating consciousness around your thinking will enable you to make changes that you desire. I believe most negative thoughts do not arise from ill intentions; they come out of habit, lack of awareness, jealousy, fear or insecurity. Thoughts can seem perfectly harmless especially when not directed outward, yet they do form life within. I put together a few questions that you can ask yourself to help create a better sense of mindfulness with your thoughts.

Answer true or false to the following questions and be completely honest with yourself.

1. I often think or verbalize that I'm tired, stressed out, overwhelmed or annoyed?

2. I will chime in on other people's gossip, negative energy or complaining?

3. I often say to myself, "I wish I would _____, but I _____."

4. I typically see what's wrong with others versus what's good?

5. I make excuses not to create change or improvement in my life?

6. I often think in terms of 'not enough' versus abundance (not enough time, sleep, money, etc.)?

7. I can feel resentful or begrudging of other's good fortune?

8. I want to do things that are creative/fun but don't?

9. I seldom do things that bring passion, excitement or joy to my relationship(s)?

10. I have a daily spiritual practice of a mantra, kindness, meditation, or contemplation?

This is not a quiz to give you a ranking score; it is an awareness measure to cue you into the energy of your life. However, what I can assure you is that your answers will demonstrate your vibrational energy. We are all responsible for our own life's energy, but most of those energies are created unconsciously. While your mind will *almost always* work subconsciously, be aware that the subconscious mind is programmed. It will go to negativity or positivity based on prior conditioning. We get used to automatic statements that live in our minds, but we can retrain the automatics.

Think about the moments in your life when you have taken the time to be in conscious thought. When you ponder deeply, pray or contemplate, energy is created inside you. There is a vibration that you feel. Your mind feels different, your heart is more tender, and your body experiences the calm. You can hold another deeply in your thoughts and believe your energy reaches out and touches them, and it does. Across the world, hundreds of millions believe in the power of prayer, meditation or just holding another tenderly in their heart. People believe in intuitive connection, soul mates, chemistry, and faith. We feel one another, read each other's expressions, draw close or move away based on eye contact, and sense danger or discomfort. All of these arise from the energy of thought which brings forth heart, soul or life to self and others.

The Heart Knows

Your heart knows when you are angry, sad, and distraught, out of sorts with yourself or others. It knows when you are silent, internalizing, and defeated. And because it knows, it produces a different rhythm in conjunction with what you feel. Your heart will beat with one rhythm when you feel at peace and content, and another when you are negative or hurting. Your heart is like an emotional thermometer for your emotional health.

Vibrating with emotion, your heart sends messages, blood and biochemicals to the brain, body and outer world. Your emotions of anger, joy, sadness, tenderness, aggression or silent suffering are felt in your heart. The rhythm of your heart feels the emotion of your life. The heart is thought to be our emotional center, or "the rhythm of life." We use terms such as our hearts are broken, we've had a change of heart, someone has a bleeding heart, and she is tender-hearted, hard-hearted and so on. These expressions have come about because when we feel emotion, we clutch our chest and recognize something different is going on with our rhythm. The sensations of thoughts are felt in the heart and create the vibrations of your life.

Think about the times when you are angry, feeling road rage, or anxiety. The heart speeds up, breathing is labored, muscles feel tense, and the vibrations of your body are stressful. You want the feeling to go away, but it won't. Desperately, you desire your heart to beat in a soothing rhythm which calms the body as though gently rocking a baby. Think about the times you and a loved one have gone to bed, hurting after an argument. The loneliness in your heart is hollow, tears roll from your cheeks and onto the sheets, and your energy is like a dead weight drawing you deeply into your mattress. All your heart desires is that your loved one put their arms around you and tell you everything's going to be all right. Just that gesture would change the weight of your body and the vibration of your heart.

When you feel loved, kindness toward another, or happy, beautiful ripples stir within your heart and move throughout your body. Tender, warm feelings, appreciation and gratitude stimulate soothing feelings to the body. Those gentle, calm feelings regulate the nervous system sending out very different vibrations to your entire body and to your outer world. The vibrations of your heart impact not only your emotional experience, but produce or enhance many of the ill effects inside the body. Studies have proven stress kills; ongoing misery in the body creates disease. Heart attacks, blood pressure, stomach and intestinal illnesses are often linked to poor emotional health. The heart's rhythm feels the unhappiness and angst of your life; the body is strained by those emotions.

We are one. Everything in our body is connected. The organs communicate with one another, the chemicals within the body are changed by our thoughts, the heart's rhythm is tempered to our emotions, and emotions reach out and touch others. We are one with our bodies, our communities and our world. What we think and do impact us and the world in which we live. We don't live in a vacuum and shouldn't, and our heart knows this. If you learn to listen, your heart will let you know when something in your life is not right. Your heart will let you know what you need in terms of closeness, space, food, laughter, movement or tenderness. The heart desires to help you cue into the needs of your mind and body. The energy of your life is based on what is going on within your body. Your happiness or unhappiness will be determined by your ability to listen to your heart.

There is a resonance within your heart that is constantly moving, inside you and out into the world. Others feel that resonance and respond to it. Your inner world and outer world are given life by the power of your essence. If you wish to change your subconscious energy, your connections or your environment, you must put your heart and focus on choosing brighter more positive energies.

Admittedly, it is not plausible that your energy is always positive, tender and forgiving. You are human, and just the experience of living in a human body will bring forth struggles, disappointment, darkness and some negativity. Hormones and body chemicals will change causing irritability, impatience, aggravation, and fatigue. Daily life will bring heartache, difficult encounters with others, frustration, sleeplessness and edginess. At times you may feel tormented by your thoughts and any efforts of optimism will be a battle. Because we are born into a feeling human body, we will experience a rise and fall of emotions. But no matter the flavor of the emotion, it is temporary. Hard emotions have a purpose. Darkness comes into our lives so that we may grow a healthier sense of compassion and consciousness, and so that we appreciate the light when it returns.

When those moments arise, humbly learn to be with them. Have self-compassion. This is not a time to sit in disappointment and judgment. Observe those moments, recognize the emotion as just that, a temporary, fleeting emotion that does not have to define you. Be forgiving of your humanness and as comforting as you would be to a young, struggling child. No one wants to feel grumpy and distraught; however, it's part of our journey. Sometimes our internal disappointment with ourselves can magnify negative feelings, and it's like pouring gasoline on burning embers. Remember the story of the two wolves; the one that wins is the one you feed. When uncomfortable feelings linger and you want them to dissipate, this could be a time for silence. Bring into your conscious awareness that this will pass. Like a bug or a virus; it's a temporary invasion of your heart. It won't last forever but continue to try to feed your life with kindness or at least tenderness.

As you evolve to cultivate mindfulness around your internal energy, remember to create awareness as to what you are being exposed to from other sources. A term I've heard a lot lately is "energy vampires." It is referencing those who suck the energy out of your life. To evolve in your own heart, there has to be consciousness around the impact to our souls by others. I want these next words to come across as tenderly and compassionately as possible. There will be people in your life that exhaust you, bring you down, and even unknowingly hurt you. You can shine your light on them and hope your rays positively impact them; however, there will be those that will not respond. There are people who will consistently zap your soul's glow, and you have to choose to create distance in order to change your vibration. It is not to say that they are bad, but perhaps unaware and unready to see the need for change in themselves. In 2009, the *New York Times* magazine ran a great article titled, "Are Your Friends Making You Fat?" The article clearly demonstrated that the people in your life help determine not only your physical health but your happiness, unhappiness and emotional health, stating that the behaviors of others are "contagious." If there is an energy vampire in your life, they will suck the happiness right out of you. They will influence your essence, your energy and your joy. However, remember that you are choosing that environment.

What You Can Do to Change your Energy

You can begin by taking accountability for what is going on in your life. Like sticky glue, your exposures cling to you and become part of who you are. Your habits, patterns, and behaviors have been learned along the way. But as you move into adulthood it is your responsibility to consciously create the life you desire. Taking responsibility for the choices of your thoughts is the beginning of the process; following through with changes in behaviors produces life-changing outcomes.

It's not easy to look at yourself and say, "I am the creator of my choices, actions, happiness or unhappiness." Conditioned, we look out into the world as victims of our own lives. We look at others as the cause of our suffering. Other's behaviors may trigger wounds that live inside you. The actions of another may create negativity, defensiveness or resentment to your very core, but you have a choice about how you respond. You also have a choice of whom and what you allow in your life. You have a choice in how you let other's words and behaviors affect you. You have a choice with your attitude, your own words, thoughts and actions.

Others will hurt you, anger and disappoint you. There is no way any of us can or will ever be so evolved that we transcend broken hearts. However, doing your soul work allows you to sit with suffering and experience transformation for having been there. Soul work is about allowing humility to live your heart. It's about taking care of you and moving away from detrimental energies. It's about realizing you don't need to win or have the last word. Soul work is learning to let things move through you and creating resiliency out of compassion, forgiveness, and self-care. You may not be able to change the world, but you can change how you are in the world.

The energy and resiliency of your life are determined by the nurturing and care of your self-worth. Taking accountability will transform your life and is also a predictor for the future of your sense of self. The less able you are to hold yourself accountable for your actions and the outcome of your life, the greater the negative impact to your self-worth. As long as you blame others, you will suffer feelings of negativity such as resentment and hostility toward another. As you continue to carry feelings of blame, doubt and resentment, your self-worth is diminished, and you will be less likely to trust or tap into your soulful or spiritual energy.

Begin to take notice of how you spend your free time, of the actions you take and the people you are bringing into your life. What you do in the present will nurture or drain your life's energy. You are feeding or depleting your mind, body and soul with the activities and surroundings of your life. Fitness, laughter, food, fun, kindness, charity, nature, music, the arts, adequate sleep, optimism, meditation, prayer, adventures, community, group activities, gratitude, intimacy, and touch are all energy towers. These things support the body, stimulate the mind and touch the soul. They feed us and make us feel the joys of our humanness.

Ask yourself what you are willing to do to change the energy of your life. Periodically, take a look at your patterns and habits and see how they are affecting you. You may hit the snooze button over and over and then wake feeling grumpy and hurried. You could choose to rise earlier and take a moment for gratitude. You may need to make amends with someone in your life. You may be participating in unknowing behaviors that create energy drains in your life. Taking responsibility will help you modify your behaviors and release negative energies that are bogging you down. Personal responsibility is the foundation for personal development; your growth and life change is dependent on it.

Exercise: Clearing Blocked Energy

- Pick an area in your life in which you are struggling. It may be that you want a healthy relationship, a new job or more education. The moment you have a defeating thought, such as, "I can't because…" say "Stop!" and replace it with optimism. "I will…"

- Focus on what your heart desires and hold that thought, not using words such as "I wish things were better" as this establishes doubt.

- Each day, wake and write your goal on a sheet of paper. For example, I will get out there and get a new job, or I will stop procrastinating, or I will work on my relationship.

- Every day, spend a few moments in silence with your eyes closed and visually see yourself achieving your goal. Picture it as though it is happening.

- Feel what it would be like to achieve that goal. Let the emotion of having what you desire wash over you as if it is occurring or has already occurred.
- Tell someone you love and trust about your goal. Put it out into the universe as this creates positive energy.
- Don't set a time limit, just stick with it.

Assume for a moment that you are both the cause and the cure for whatever is going on in your life. Your mind holds a thought about anything, and that thought will create your experience. Clearing blocked energy is about creating a new mental experience. Your brain is waiting for you to tell it what to do, and with enough time, will do exactly as you ask. Most problems or roadblocks are created within the focus of your attention, and most can be resolved with a different set of thoughts.

Chapter Ten

The Soul Waits

"The soul is an infinite ocean of just beautiful energy and presence made manifest in human form." — Panache Desai

These bodies that we occupy are miraculous—and powerful. Your body, functioning from the communication of trillions of cells, will thrive or deteriorate based on your choices. Your body has a brain, a mind, a will and a soul. To not recognize the power you have within you is a misfortune, literally a missed fortune. You can have a strong thought, and that thought will enforce a feeling because the chemicals in your body produced in response to that thought. Then you will take action and your life will take form, and it all began with a thought.

We aren't taught in simple terms how to put it all together, not because it's too complex to understand, but because it's too amazing to actually believe. We're skeptical about the strength we have within ourselves, which isn't a bad thing; it makes us question and search. As you search and grow, to know and understand yourself and your body, you know what feels authentically true. You know it all works together, and it's all based on you. It's not to blame yourself for the aches, pain, sorrows and failures in your life. It is to recognize, in spite of those things, you have capabilities beyond what you can imagine. Of course, you are going to be ill, get diseases and pass from this life. You are going to be stressed beyond what feels within your control. Unpredictable life events are going to catch you off guard, and your thoughts and emotions will thrust you into a whirlwind. However, you have the resources to re-ground yourself, to come back to your center, to move through whatever is going on, and to make changes for an optimum life experience.

I worked with a woman, not yet fifty years old, on issues of codependency, internal resentment, and feelings of powerlessness. She had been my client for some time when she walked into my office and said, "I have been diagnosed with cancer." Jane, physically fit, loved the outdoors and had an overall pleasant attitude about life. However, her story revolved around not listening to her soul. She stayed in a silent, passive-aggressive, unhappy marriage, she allowed family members to dominate her time and energy and felt guilty whenever she thought about doing what she needed for herself.

Jane's second sentence was, "I know I did this to myself; I know it in my heart." Her journey for the next couple of years would be surgery, treatment for cancer and intensive internal personal work. Before Jane went for her surgery, this is what she had to say.

"I get it now, I really do. It's odd; I'm not frightened at all; I'm not worried. I know I'm gonna be okay. It may sound crazy, but I think this cancer is a gift. It's like I can almost see and feel this toxic ball of misery that has been my emotional life for so long. I kinda knew it was happening; I just couldn't get myself to stop. God—I

lived my life knotted up inside trying so hard to make everything okay for everybody. And even when I would feel sad and exhausted, I thought it made me a better, stronger person to suck it up. It's no wonder I got sick, but I'm gonna be okay, I just know I am."

Jane found her voice, left her marriage, set boundaries with her children and extended family, and discovered beautiful ways in which to love life and take care of herself. She dug deep and did her soul work. She found her strength by learning to listen to her inner voice. Years later she is cancer-free; at times still struggling, but overall healthy and happy. The difference is she is now able to sit with her sorrows, work through them and come out on the other side.

Growing the Soul

The soul waits for us to grow into our potential. It waits for us to recognize the difference between our inner voice and those inner voices that have been programmed from someone else. It waits for us to grow past our wounds of defensiveness, anger, blame, fear, doubt and insecurity; and it is there for us whenever we need it. Though sometimes not so easy to hear and recognize, it's always there. The subtle insight that shows itself in dreams, anxious feelings, questions, passion, desire, uneasiness, and intuition is the soul's voice. The soul won't drag you kicking and screaming into awakening. However, sometimes life does for us what we are not capable of doing ourselves. Natural pain and suffering will push us into growth. You may get fired from that job you've been declaring you'll quit. You may get bedridden with illness, lose a loved one, or just lay in angst, night after night, unable to sleep. The soul waits for us to grow up enough to take responsibility for our own lives, for us to listen to our instincts, and to create the life and peace that we desire.

Growing up is about realizing things won't always go your way, life is fragile, and emotions are scary. It's about learning compassion and forgiveness for others because no matter what we think we know; we don't know the whole story. There are always two sides to every tale. Most of the sayings taught to us through the wisdom of our grandmothers are true; you can catch more flies with honey than vinegar, and life is not fair. Growing up is about realizing these bodies are amazing, but with time will fail us, so we need not take them for granted. They need as much tender love and care as possible. People will disappoint us; they will break our hearts, not because they are evil or ill-intended, but because they too are struggling with fractured hearts and trying to figure out how to grow up. Forgiveness is not a luxury; it's a necessity. Wounded hearts are not the toxins that wreak havoc on our emotions, holding onto resentments—the inability to let go is what will poison a life.

Growing up is about awakening to the vastness of everything; realizing we are connected, and all of our actions eventually return to us. We grow to identify that we have needs, but we are not the center of the universe. When we become capable of seeing life as bigger than ourselves, we become able to give to others, and this helps us identify our own needs and how to get them met through healthy methods that lift us up instead of tearing us down. Emotional disasters become less enticing, and emotional maturity is a little more desirable. Hopefully, there comes a point when we realize growing up is not so bad. Being the creator of our destinies, forming our own lives, choosing our thoughts is a gift. Embracing equality, humility, integrity, accountability and compassion, opens the heart a bit wider, allows a life to be lived a lot larger and gives the soul a chance to emerge and develop an adult heart within these shells we call bodies.

When I was in my mid-twenties an older, and much wiser, friend of mine said, "Often in my life when I am struggling or trying to make decisions, I look around the room and wonder when the grown-ups are going to show up and fix my life." I clearly remember thinking that was odd; being in my twenties and naive, I was sure I was finally the grown-up. In hindsight, this lingered in my mind because of the incredible vulnerability and truth of her statement. So many times I have desperately wished a grown-up would show up and take over my life. With the passage of time, I have evolved to realize, we spend our lives growing up a little more each day; feeling insecure, being afraid, making mistakes, figuring out how to take responsibility, working through heartache, embracing loneliness, learning how to forgive one another, and accepting the vulnerability of this life. As we grow, hopefully, we soften toward ourselves and humanity. And as we soften, accountability and compassion become the cornerstone of our lives.

Through the years, clients have been some of my greatest teachers in awakening and understanding the human soul. I see good people desperately trying to figure out life, wanting to love, be loved, to find peace and happiness. I see clients battle with their pasts, struggle with their future; humans riddled with addictions, broken hearts, angry, abused, diseased, abandoned and lost, wrestling with emotions they don't understand. They follow paths that have been laid before them thinking they are helpless to do things differently. I am humbled, as I have had the honor of looking inside those hearts and seeing a vulnerability that is rarely shared. And through the looking glass of so many souls, I have seen humans beautiful beyond explanation. I have seen the guarded let their guard down, exposing raw stunning emotions; the defenseless disclosing shame, desperation and humiliation. I have sat with the angry, scared, tender, weak and weary, all softened by honesty and connection with the soul. And from that, I have learned. I have become a better me because I have seen the capabilities of the soul.

Your Soul's Destiny

Doing your soul work is the most important work you will do in this life. It isn't something you do once, and it's done; it's an ongoing process of growth, development, opportunity and gifts. With each life milestone, you change. You know a bit more than you knew before. You become more alive and awake. You feel a new level of depth; you are no longer the same. Your soul develops and becomes stronger as you develop and grow stronger. Your soul's destiny is that you don't stay the same, but that you remain in the process of growing with your life.

Your journey is like a set of stairs you are climbing with lots of floors on which to stop. It's easy to rest at one level and get really comfortable staying in one place. You familiarize yourself with everything at that level. You surround yourself with others who are also at that level. The longer you stay there, the harder it is for you and your soul to grow. You may become complacent, losing sight of life's beautiful opportunities, challenging yourself less, more avoidant or fearful and slowly losing sight of the climb—until life shakes you up. It shakes you up sometimes by internal restlessness and sometimes external suffering. As it shakes you up, you have a choice; you can move up a few more steps, or you can resist the call. Your climb is based on your emotional maturity.

When you are ready to climb again, you may meet resistance from those around you. You may even have to leave a few relationships behind because, as you climb, not everyone in your circle will understand or be ready to make the climb with you. Fear will set in, and even the thought of loneliness can convince you to stay in your comfortable circle of life; however, the choice is yours. This is where emotional maturity and self-care are incredibly important as they will give you the strength to go it alone when you have to. And as you go it alone, you are not really alone as there are many other souls evolving at the same pace and willing to out-stretch a hand when you need it.

As you climb, you will come to another floor, gravity will set in, and you will remain there for a while. It will be only a matter of time before the need to journey on will occur. The motivation to climb will not always be prompted by huge life events. You will evolve as you read a new book with awakening information. You will evolve as you realize the need for improved self-care, or through the simple process of aging. Your growth on the evolutionary scale of life will consist of everything from meeting a new friend who makes you want to travel more, or facing a tragic death of someone you love dearly. You will do new things, hopefully, travel to new places, work through grief, and gravity will almost certainly settle you back into a slumber. It is not to judge or condemn yourself for those times of living in your comfort zone, but recognize the need in your body and soul to continue to move forward on the beautiful journey that life will place before you.

Sometimes humans are frustrated by the perceived expectation that we are to keep growing and striving. Depending on how you view the world, it could seem as though it is a never-ending journey. But once you are able to change your thoughts, you can see that is our truest gift of life. We don't remain the same; we have the ability to bounce back, and we are always capable of the climb. We have the feelings that we have, so we desire, yearn, reach and strive. We can taste new things, see beautiful, breathtaking places, create new pieces of art, laugh and love again. No matter how many times I see the Southwest, it takes my breath away. The Canadian Rockies are spectacular, the Smokey Mountains instill awe, and the ocean never grows old. When we get our hearts broken, we can love again. When we feel like we can't breathe because our children grow up and leave our homes, we can begin again. We can choose to remain open, recreate ourselves and climb to the next floor in life.

It's never over until we no longer occupy these bodies; even then none of us know for sure. But as long as we do, we have a spiritual responsibility to live as fully alive as possible. It doesn't mean you always have to travel to new places and do new things. It doesn't mean life has to be filled with exotic changes and grand gestures. It simply means you always need to be alive, that is your soul's destiny. Physically moving your body, meditating, having coffee with a friend, sitting by a fire or cuddling with your children—when done in consciousness means you are alive. Knowing what you need when you need it, taking accountability, listening to your soul and being willing to take the next step when it's time, means you are alive. Not taking this life for granted, or expecting constant ease along the way means you are alive. And you can remain alive and move up the steps of life by creating mindfulness and consciously choosing to live wide awake.

Practice Love

The very best way to acknowledge the soul and to remain awake is through the path of love. The soul, though it experiences the sum of everything, is pure love. We are cautious with our love, yet always trying to find ways to love and be loved. It is the essence of our being. I will state again and again that we are either operating out of fear or out of love, and I will take it a step further. We operate out of fear because we are so desiring of, and wanting to feel connected and to be loved.

If you desire to live a richer life, make it a point to practice love as deeply and as often as possible. Love is the soul's language. Love who you are, what you do, and as many people as you possibly can. Love the sunrise and sunset, the mornings, winter, spring and fall. Love opportunities, laughter, giving, togetherness and even difficulties. There isn't another thing on this planet as gratifying as love. When clients ask if I know what love is, my answer is always the same.

"Love is patient, love is kind. It does not envy, it does not boast, it is not proud. It does not dishonor others, it is not self-seeking, it is not easily angered, it keeps no record of wrongs. Love does not delight in evil but rejoices with the truth. It always protects, always trusts, always hopes, always perseveres."

— 1 Corinthians 13:4-6

Love yourself enough so that when you look out into the world, you are looking through the eyes of love. When deep love is lived inside you, your view of the world is more loving. As you love, you will be fully alive, fully moved and dedicated to the growth of your life, and to the love and growth of those around you. Grow to understand that you, your choices, your emotions and your health are interconnected with every other human in your life experience. We are "one" with ourselves, one with another and one with this planet. The greater the divisiveness, the greater the suffering will be. Everything that positions itself to work together creates a higher performing system. We need connectivity in our bodies, minds, and souls—and we need one another.

Love is a soul energy that resonates outward and will be returned inward. The ability to love your life, yourself and others will be achieved through the choices you make. See the person you desire to be and create it, beginning with the energy of your thoughts. Practice the life you desire and love as often as possible; even in the harder moments of your life. Being human isn't always easy, with all of our moods, wounds and emotions—but in spite of the difficulties, it can be a beautiful journey. There is no greater way to live this life than through that of a loving heart.

Sometimes I look at the stars, the moon or the ocean in pure bewilderment. Spinning at thousands of miles per hour, perfectly balanced in the darkness of space, tiny little fragments— and still, we exist. Being human is miraculous, amazing beyond conception. We get to love, laugh, and cry, feel pain and utter ecstasy—all because we possess these brilliantly, wonderful, confusing human bodies and souls. The busyness of life makes us forget, touching one another's souls helps us remember.

Rules for Being a Happy Human

By Tamela Duncan

1. You will receive a body, a mind and a soul. And you get to choose how you live in them.

2. No one can or will live your life for you, even though at times some may try.

3. You have worth far beyond what you have ever been told; believe it.

4. There will be joy available to you. It won't show up on your doorstep; you have to go out there and get it.

5. You will suffer, and you will learn from that suffering—if you don't take on the victim role.

6. In time you will find there is nothing better than having a compassionate heart.

7. Your thoughts will hurt you or help you; choose them wisely.

8. Small joys become big joys when you stop taking life for granted and live in gratitude.

9. You will vacillate between love and fear. Make a conscious effort to always return to love.

10. The outcome of your life, health and happiness are in your hands. It's a big responsibility, so take it seriously.

30 Days to Emotional Mind Change

"I believe that we learn by practice. Whether it means to learn to dance by practicing dancing or to learn to live by practicing living, the principles are the same." — *Martha Graham*

All change takes time. It takes time to lose weight, time to learn a new language or to save for a new automobile. It takes time for the brain to change and time for you to learn that you can change. You are a product of whatever you consistently practice, no matter what those practices may be. Change does not occur simply through your body and brain working for you. It occurs through you, working for you. So, for thirty days incorporate these practices; make choices that make you better.

1. Wake each morning and acknowledge three things for which you are grateful. If you are suffering and having a hard time with gratitude, simply be grateful that you have water, or limbs that function or eyes that see—but be grateful.

2. Reach out to others. Don't always go it alone. Find a confidant, get a good therapist, or become part of a group; gain the support you need in healing, setting goals, or becoming a better person. There is no greater investment in this life than your mental health. "Surround yourself with dreamers and doers, the believers and thinkers, but most of all surround yourself with

those who see greatness within you, even when you don't see it in yourself." Unknown.

3. Find books that speak the language of loving kindness, forgiveness, healing, change and personal growth. If you can do no more than reading one page or one paragraph per day, that's okay. But read, for your own personal development.

4. Write affirmations for yourself and your life. Affirm that which needs to be affirmed. Example: May I be peaceful, loving and kind. May I see the beauty in all that surrounds me. May I open my heart to love myself and others. May I be peaceful, loving and kind.

5. Laughter—simple and beautiful—is one of life's greatest medicines; make sure you do this often. Allow yourself to have fun, seek opportunities that make you laugh and feel like a kid again. It's okay to be a little silly, to laugh out loud, to be filled with excitement, and feel the pleasures of simple things.

6. Have a plan to physically move your body for twenty to thirty minutes each day. If you feel that you can't exercise every day, then exercise every other day, but start. Find what works for you. If one type of exercise does not feel good, try another and another until something works.

7. Begin the practice of meditation. Look in your area for available classes. If there are none available to you, purchase meditations on CDs or downloads. As you start this practice be patient and kind with yourself. Even if you feel you are not getting it, stick with it—it takes time. Try to meditate ten to

twenty minutes each day. If you feel you cannot manage this practice daily, then try it every other day, or three times a week. This is an acquired skill as we are not used to quieting our minds—have patience.

8. Recognize the food, toxins, sugars and artificial sweeteners that you are putting into your body. I am not asking for drastic changes—just limitations. Get rid of things that weigh you down or make you feel poorly in your skin. Nurture your body through what you consume.

9. Live in consciousness; you are your thoughts. Thoughts trigger your mind and form pathways in your brain, which eventually become your automatic responses. Learn to live in mindfulness and choose your thoughts.

10. Learn to love yourself deeply. Let go of old wounds. Forgive people, whether you feel they deserve to be forgiven or not. You deserve to stop carrying it around. You can love yourself deeply by releasing old, harmful ways of being.

11. Introduce a new hobby, skill or talent in your life. Take up tennis, tai chi, yoga, playing the guitar or learning to paint. Don't begin these practices to be good, or to compete, rather do them for enjoyment. They will enhance your brain and add something new and pleasurable to your life.

12. Before you close your eyes each night, acknowledge three things that were good in your day. They don't have to be major things, just little things. If you look for the positives that surround you, more and more of them will become noticeable.

Made in the USA
Columbia, SC
31 March 2019